The World of the Arts

The World of the Arts

by

FRED LOGAN
Art Educator

MARCELLA O'LEARY
Music Educator

PAUL GAUGER
Speech Educator

ANNE NEIGOFF, *Managing Editor*

Illustrations by Katherine Grace, Luther Johnson, Frank C. Murphy, Don Loehle, Howard Simon, Phero Thomas

Special Advisor: Virgil Herrick

STANDARD EDUCATIONAL CORPORATION *Chicago 1985*

Library of Congress Cataloging in Publication Data
Logan, Frederick M
    The world of the arts.

    1. Arts—Juvenile literature.
    I. O'Leary, Marcella, joint author.
    II. Gauger, Paul, 1914-   joint author.
    III. Grace, Katherine, illus.
    IV. Title.

NX633.L63   700'.9   74-12311
ISBN 0-87392-306-0

You are about to begin on a voyage of discovery to a world of wonder and surprise. It is a world that is as old as the cave man and as young as tomorrow. You will not find this world on any map. It has no boundaries, north or south, east or west. Yet people of all countries have journeyed there.

In this world there are wonderful things to see—paintings that glow with color, strange masks from far-off lands, buildings of ageless splendor, and many other shapes and forms.

There are wonderful things to hear—songs to sing and music to play. Minstrel songs and symphonies fill the air with the sounds of music.

There are plays and actors of many kinds. Clowns strut upon a stage to make us laugh. A ship sails away to hunt for a pirate treasure. Shadows talk and puppets dance for our pleasure.

Rembrandt and Michelangelo belong to this world. Beethoven and Shakespeare are part of it. An unknown potter in ancient Greece, an Indian who carved a war club long ago, and perhaps you, yourself, belong to it, too.

For the world we will explore is the world of the arts, and there are many kinds of arts and artists. Each artist works in a different way to tell the story of the world he knows or imagines.

Some artists use words to tell a story. Other artists use a picture or a carving or the sounds of music. All artists use the language of the arts—a language that people of every time and in every country have understood and loved.

As you adventure with us through the wonderful world of the arts, we hope that you will learn to love and understand and use that language, too.

Table of Contents

Full-Color Reproductions

Music to Sing and Play

If you could go walking one day and meet a cave boy and girl who lived thousands and thousands of years ago, how would you talk to them?

You could not use words, for they would not understand. You could not say, "Let's be friends. Tell me all about how you lived. Was it fun to live in a cave? Were you afraid when you saw the huge mammoth? How brave your hunters were to face him with a flint knife and a throwing dart for weapons!"

But you could talk to them without words.

You could draw a picture of your house to say, "This is where I live." The cave girl could draw a picture of her cave. The cave boy could draw a picture of a hunter and a charging mammoth.

He could beat his chest and shout triumphantly to tell you that the hunter had conquered the mammoth. That would be the cave man's way of singing his victory song, and as you listened, you would understand, for people have always made music to express triumph and pride, joy and sadness, hope and prayer.

You could not speak together in words, but you could smile and act out the story that you wanted to be friends.

If you met a boy from Norway or Japan, you probably could not speak to them with words. But you could still talk together.

You and the cave boy and girl are thousands of years apart. You and the boy from Norway or Japan are thousands of miles apart. But you could speak to each other through a picture, a song, or a play—through art and music and drama. For these are a language that people of every time and in every country have known and understood and loved.

11

A picture has been said to be something between

In the Omnibus
Mary Cassatt (1845–1926) American

Artists have always made pictures
of the things they know
and love and imagine. Sometimes
they draw the picture.
What kind of story does this
drawing by Mary Cassatt
tell you?

Sometimes an artist paints
his picture. This *Little Girl
in Pantalettes* was painted
by an unknown American artist
in the nineteenth century.
Can you tell the ways
it is different from
the drawing at the left?

Art

a thing and a thought —SAMUEL PALMER

Courtesy of Mr. and Mrs. Samuel A. Marx

Man on a Horse
Marino Marini (1901–1980) Italian

Sometimes an artist carves
or models a figure. Sculpture
is different from a drawing
or a painting. It is a solid
form. You want to touch it
and feel its surfaces. You
can walk around it and see
how it looks different from
different views.

Some artists make the things
we use and wear. They know
that a pitcher that holds milk
can have a graceful shape
and a pleasing design. Artists
make pictures in many different
ways, but each artist tries
to create a picture
in his own way, as he sees it.

13

DRAWING

Lines on Snow and Paper

ERARLY one winter morning a boy arose and looked out of his window. There was snow on the ground, deep and powdery. The trees, the street and houses in the distance, the whole countryside were covered with a white blanket of snow.

On the ground were signs that earlier risers had been out. The boy could read the story in the lines on the snow. Rabbit tracks had made a path that curved beyond the bare lilac bushes. Narrow ruts showed where a milk truck had crossed from one side of the street to the other.

Dressing quickly, the boy ran outside. Suddenly a dog barked, and a rabbit dashed across the yard to hide in the bushes. The dog jumped into the deep snow as it chased the rabbit. Both the dog and the rabbit made new prints in the snow.

As the boy walked across the snowy yard, he made a fresh track of his own.

The tracks on the snow are like lines drawn on paper by an artist. They make a picture. They tell a story.

The tracks tell us who made them. A rabbit, a dog, and a boy make different kinds of prints on the snow.

The tracks tell us something else. As the frightened rabbit dashed across the snow, he made a different kind of track from the even, unhurried rabbit path that curved beyond the lilac bushes. His leaping tracks told the story of his fear.

The lines in a picture tell us a story, too. They also tell us something about the artist who drew the picture. They tell us how he felt about the thing he drew. They tell us what kind of tools he used to draw the picture.

The Artist's Tools

WHAT tools does an artist use to make a picture? Suppose you want to make a picture. What will you use? You can use many things. Each tool you use will make a different kind of line.

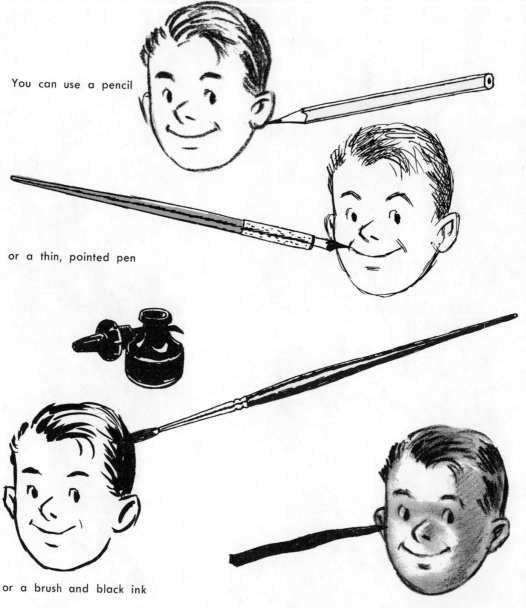

You can use a pencil

or a thin, pointed pen

or a brush and black ink

or a black stick of charcoal

The artist
who drew
this picture
used
colored pastels
to tell
her story.

Courtesy Dr. and Mrs. Walter Greenson

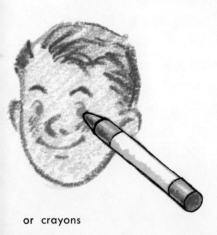

or crayons

or colored chalks

17

Draw a Picture of Your Own

T HE tools an artist uses are important because each tool makes a different kind of picture. More important still is the person who draws the picture.

If you and the boy next door and the girl across the street each drew a picture of the same house, each picture would be just a little different from the other pictures. If your little brother or sister drew that same house, we would have still another kind of picture of that house. For each of us sees things just a little differently. The pictures we draw show this.

Probably, however, you would not all want to draw the same house. What an artist chooses to draw also tells something about him.

What kind of pictures do you like to draw? Do you like to draw real things or pretend things? Do you like to draw pictures of things you know or pictures of things you would like to see and know?

If you live near the ocean, do you like to draw a picture like the one of the fishermen and their boat? Would you rather draw a picture of mountains or of the sandy desert?

The girl who drew the picture near her school wanted to draw something she knew. If you were drawing a picture of your school, would you want to put the same things in your picture that she put in her picture?

What colors do you like to use in your pictures? Do you like some colors better than others? What kind of shapes do you like to draw?

Every time you draw a picture, you tell something about yourself. You tell something about the kind of person you are. You tell something, too, of how you are feeling when you draw the picture.

If you are happy, your picture will be different from the picture you draw when you are sad or angry. Next time you draw a picture, look at it and see if you can tell what it is saying about you.

Remember that each of us should choose the kind of picture he wants to draw. Each of us should draw the picture as he sees it. That is the only good way to draw a picture.

A Haul from the Chesapeake Bay
Grade 7, Norfolk, Virginia

Scene Near Elizabeth School
Grade 4, Charlotte, North Carolina

In how many ways are the two pictures on this page different from each other? What does each tell about the artist who drew it? Are the pictures alike in any ways? Are they like a picture you drew one day? Are they like a picture you would like to draw?

Tommy Logan

Growing Things
Grade 7, Madison, Wisconsin

Arts and Activities' Third Biennial Exhibition of American Child Art

What do the pictures on these pages tell you about the artists who drew them? What do they make you feel?

At the Movies
Grade 5, Milwaukee, Wisconsin

An Artist and His Picture

THERE are many kinds of pictures. There are pictures of people and of places and of things. Each picture tells us about the artist who drew it. Often an artist draws a picture of something he knows. His picture tells us what he saw and how he saw it. It may tell us, too, where and when he lived.

Do you live in the country? If you do, many of the things you see and do belong to the countryside. If you draw a picture of a country scene, your picture will tell that you are drawing something you know.

20

Your picture will tell where you live. It may tell, too, about the time in which you are living. A picture of the country today will be different from a picture of the country years ago when there were no tractors in the fields.

A city boy can draw a picture of the country, too, as he saw it on vacation or as he imagines it. His picture will be different from your picture of the country. The things he chooses to draw probably will be different. The way he sees the things probably will be different, too.

His picture may make you want to laugh or it may make you feel proud of the place where you live. It may make you look around with surprise, for the things that are old to you may be new and exciting and wonderful to him.

For an artist draws not only what he sees, but what he feels about people and places and things. As we look at a picture, we share something of the artist's feeling.

Sometimes an artist draws something he knows and loves. Sometimes he draws something he remembers or imagines. Always he helps us see and understand the wonder and beauty of the world around us.

Arts and Activities' Third Biennial Exhibition of American Child Art

The Big Fire
Grade 7, Louisville, Kentucky

Kodachrome by Romain Robert, President of the Société Prehistorique de L'Ariege

This drawing was found on the wall of a cave in Lascaux, France. The animal figures were partly drawn, partly cut into the rock. Do you see how the power and movement of the animals make them seem almost alive?

Cave Drawings

PEOPLE have been drawing pictures for thousands and thousands of years. The first people to draw pictures had no written language. Yet just like you, they wanted to tell a story about the things they saw and the way they lived.

Twenty-five thousand years ago, cave men drew pictures on the walls of their caves to tell how they hunted the bison, rhinoceros, and the charging mammoth. They used pieces of red and yellow ocher for chalk. They used sharp flint points to cut lines into the rock walls.

Today we can still see their drawings on the walls of caves in France and Spain. What story does the cave-man drawing on this page tell you?

Like the cave men, other people who lived long ago used pictures instead of words to tell a story or send a message.

Egyptian Drawings

This is an Egyptian picture writing of an alphabet sign or letter.

THE EARLY Egyptians used pictures to show a sign of the alphabet or a syllable in a word. For many years men puzzled over the drawings they found on the walls of ancient Egyptian temples and pyramids. Then, in 1799, a huge flat stone was discovered near the city of Rosetta in Egypt. On one side of the Rosetta stone were Egyptian drawings, and on the other side was the very same message in Greek. Each Greek word stood for an Egyptian symbol. By comparing the familiar Greek language with the unknown Egyptian signs and symbols, men gradually learned to read the ancient language of the people of the Nile.

The Metropolitan Museum of Art

Musicians
Egyptian (1400 B.C.)

This is an ancient Egyptian drawing. The Egyptians did not make action drawings like the cave men did. They liked to make beautiful designs and they usually drew flat, side-view pictures.

An Artist Draws Space

Look at the pictures on this page. They are different in many ways. Can you tell one important difference between them?

The drawing by Claude Lorrain shows people and trees against a faraway background. It gives you a feeling of space, or *perspective*. Perspective is the art of drawing things as they look to the eye.

The buffalo skin picture has no sense of space, or perspective. Things close and things far away are the same size.

The Pierpont Morgan Library

Sermon on the Mount
Claude Lorrain (1600–1682) French

Many years ago a Pawnee Indian drew this picture on a buffalo skin. Can you tell what the men on horseback are doing? Indians often drew pictures to send a message or tell a story.

24

Smithsonian Institution

You can see an example of perspective when you look at train tracks that stretch far into the distance. As the tracks stretch farther and farther away, they look as if they were coming together, or *converging,* in the distance.

How can you get perspective into your drawings? Use lines that come together, or converge, to get a sense of distance. Use lighter lines to show things that are far away. Use darker lines to draw things that are near. Remember that things drawn large look close. Things drawn small look far away.

It was only about five hundred years ago that artists began to learn how to show space in their pictures and draw what we call landscapes. An artist should know about perspective, but he does not have to use it in every drawing. An artist should draw a picture as he sees it.

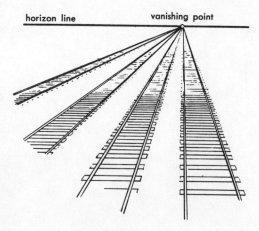

horizon line   vanishing point

Pen and Ink Drawings

Dᴵᴰ you ever make a drawing with pen and ink? Some artists like to use pen and ink when they make drawings that look like patterns. Ben Shahn did that in his picture "Still Music." Do you see how the thin pen lines are just right to make us feel how light and easily tipped the chairs and music stands are?

Paul Klee used a fine pen line to draw his gay, make-believe drawing of ghosts. Do you think he had fun drawing this picture?

Artists use pen and ink, too, when they draw the funny joke pictures, or cartoons, we see in newspapers and magazines. Did you ever see "Dennis, the Menace" in your newspaper?

There are many ways to make drawings. We can use pencil or pen, a stick of charcoal or a brush and ink, colored chalk or crayon. We can draw pictures with or without perspective. We can draw places or people or things. But we should always remember to draw a picture as we see it. For each of us sees things in a different way. That is one reason drawing is fun!

Phillips Collection

Still Music
Ben Shahn (1898–1969) American

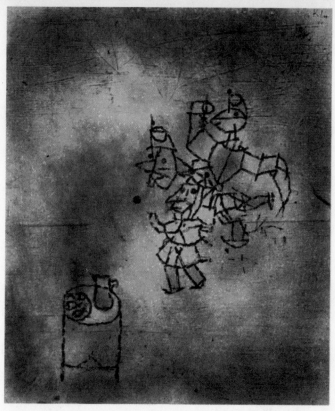

Starving Spirits
Paul Klee (1879–1940) Swiss

"YOU WANNA KNOW SOMETHIN'? YOU CAN'T SWIM IN MUD!"

Hank Ketcham is the artist who draws "Dennis, the Menace," and makes us laugh at the funny things Dennis does and says. Did you ever try to draw a cartoon?

PAINTING

Exploring the World of Color

Do you like surprises and adventures? Would you like to go on a voyage of discovery? Then try painting!

You won't need seven-league boots or a space ship. All you will need is paint and brush and paper and an eager curiosity. And off you will go to explore new worlds of color and form and composition and design.

Look at the painting of St. George and the Dragon. Then look at a black-and-white drawing or a color drawing. What differences can you see?

National Gallery of Art, Mellon Collection, Washington, D. C.

St. George and the Dragon
Raphael (1483—1520) Italian

This painting by Raphael tells the story of St. George and how he killed the dragon and saved the lovely princess. Raphael painted this picture before he was twenty-two years old. He was already a master painter, yet his later paintings show how he continued to learn as he worked. An artist grows as he tries new ways and new ideas.

Yellow and red make orange.

Yellow and blue make green.

Blue and red make purple.

Adventures with Paint

Paint is not like pencil or chalk or crayon. It is wet. You can make exciting discoveries with paint.

You can use a paint color alone, or you can mix it with another color and make a new color.

You can mix your colors before you dip your brush into the paint. Or you can put one stroke of color on the paper, and, while it is still wet, paint on another color. The two wet colors will run together and make something new.

You can put a stroke of color on your paper, let it dry, and then paint another color over it lightly. This will make another new color.

Colors are exciting in another way. Did you ever think about how different colors make you feel? When you look at red, do you feel warm or cold? Do you feel sad or gay? Do you feel excited or do you feel sleepy?

When you look at blue, how do you feel? At orange? Green?

You will find that different colors can make a painting seem peaceful or lonely, joyous or angry. Try them!

Red, orange, and yellow
are warm colors.

Blues, blue-greens,
and blue-purples are
cool colors.

Some colors—like yellow-green and purple and
brown—are combinations of warm and cool colors.

You can make exciting discoveries with a brush, too. Some brushes are stiff. Some bend and spread. You can make them move fast or slowly. You can press down hard or brush the paper lightly.

Do you wonder that artists have always made paintings of the things they knew and loved and remembered and imagined? Can you imagine how it would be if there were no pictures in books or magazines for you to look at and enjoy?

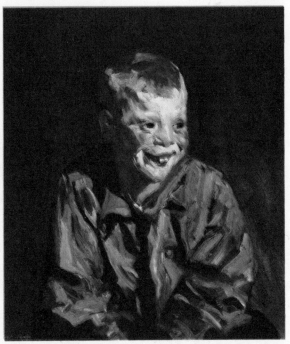

Milwaukee Art Center

Dutch Joe
Robert Henri (1865–1929) American

You can paint boldly with
slashing brush strokes and a thick
coating of paint as in this picture.

Art Institute of Chicag

Austrian Tyrol
John Marin (1870–1953) American

You can paint lightly with
delicate brush strokes and a thin
coating of paint as in this watercolor.
A watercolor may be a delicate
picture or a bold picture. Do you
see how the color changes as you
paint lightly or boldly?

This illuminated page is from a manuscript written in the sixteenth century. Do you see how carefully and beautifully each letter was formed? Notice the delicate details in the pictures that border the page.

Hours of the Virgin
(16th Century) Tours, France

Illuminated Books and Woodcuts

Hundreds of years ago, few people could read or write. There were only a few books, and they were usually made by monks in monasteries. Each book was written by hand, and the monks decorated, or *illuminated,* the letters with scarlet and gold paints. Often they painted pictures along the borders of the pages of the books to make them beautiful.

Later men began to print books. First they used wooden blocks, and carved the letters and the pictures on the wood by hand. In the fifteenth century, printers began to use movable type. But the pictures in the books were still small and crude and cut in wood.

Giotto was one of the first of
the famous mural painters of Italy.
He was one of the first, too,
to try to draw people as they really
are. This was a new idea, and
his figures may seem a little stiff
to us, for he had to learn many
new ways of drawing. This painting
is one of a group he did in the
Arena Chapel in Padua, Italy, to
tell the story of the life of Christ.
Can you tell what part of the story
this picture shows?

Photo Alinari

Flight into Egypt
Giotto (1276?–?1337) Italian

The Renaissance and Painting

IN THE fourteenth century a new interest in painting, sculpture, and architecture began and lasted into the sixteenth century. This period is called the Renaissance. There were few books or printed pictures during this time, but there were many beautiful paintings. Kings and rich nobles ruled the lands. They built magnificent palaces and wanted paintings to decorate them. Churches and cathedrals were rising. Architects and sculptors and painters were needed to make them beautiful.

It was a golden age for painting—the age of Raphael and Leonardo da Vinci and Michelangelo. Painters were given honor and wealth. Often they lived in the palace of a king or a noble or of the Pope himself. They had many pupil-assistants, or apprentices, to study under them. Best of all, they were making new discoveries about painting.

They were learning to use perspective, or space, in painting. They were discovering how a real figure stands and moves. Often they painted murals, or wall-pictures, on the wall of a palace or church, and this led to a new way of painting.

34

The artists of the Renaissance painted their murals in fresco, brushing paint directly on the wet plaster of a wall. The paint and plaster dried almost instantly to form a hard, lasting coating, so the artists had to paint swiftly. They discovered that they could not use tiny details. They had to think of the picture as it would look as part of the wall, and then paint it as a whole. They had to use colors that could be seen from a distance. Even today, many of these fresco paintings show colors as clear and brilliant as when the artist painted them.

Photo Alinari

The Holy Family
Michelangelo (1475–1564) Italian

Michelangelo was one of the geniuses of the Renaissance. He was a sculptor and architect as well as a great painter. He painted this picture about two hundred years after Giotto lived. Can you see how painting changed in that time? Giotto's figures seem a little stiff. Michelangelo's figures seem almost alive. Yet Michelangelo liked to think of himself as a sculptor, not a painter. He painted his famous frescos in the ceiling of the Sistine Chapel only because he was ordered to by Pope Julius II.

Painting Reflects the Way We Live

Aʀᴛɪsᴛs are always finding new ways of painting a picture. They are always finding new things to paint. That is one of the wonderful things about painting. It changes as the life of the people changes.

After the Renaissance, kings and nobles began to lose some of their power. Busy, thriving towns and cities began to grow. Artists began to look at the people around them and paint pictures the people wanted to see.

They began to paint the ways in which people lived. They painted people at home.

National Gallery of Art, Widener Collection, Washington, D. C.

The Bedroom
Pieter de Hooch (1629–after 1677) Dutch

Does this painting make you think of your own bedroom and of watching your mother make the bed? Do you see how the sunlight falls through the window and how the artist has made you see space within space?

They painted people at work.

The Cook
Jan Vermeer (1632–1675) Dutch

This artist painted a woman at work. In this painting by Jan Vermeer we see a Dutch peasant girl pouring milk from a pitcher. Do you notice how you can almost feel the rough, coarse weave of the girl's bodice? You can almost touch the crusty loaves of bread!

Rijks Museum, Amsterdam

Rijks Museum, Amsterdam

The Syndics
Rembrandt (1606–1669) Dutch

The businessmen of Rembrandt's time liked to have their pictures painted as a group. This painting shows the syndics, or officers, of the Drapers' Guild in Amsterdam seated about a table. Do you see how Rembrandt used shadowy darkness at the bottom of the painting to make us look up at the brightly lighted faces and hands of the men?

37

Artists painted children at play . . .

they painted the green rolling countryside . . .

. . . and the surging sea.

The Kunsthistorisches Museum, Vienna

Children's Games
Pieter Brueghel the Elder (1520?–1569) Flemish

It is about four hundred years since Pieter Brueghel painted these children of
Belgium and Holland at play. Today, if you paint a picture of your school
playground, how many boys and girls will still be playing ball or leapfrog
or having a tug of war?

National Gallery of Art, Widener Collection, Washington, D. C.

Wivenhoe Park, Essex
John Constable (1776–1837) English

John Constable is one of the most famous English landscape painters.
Do you see how the color of the trees and the water changes as the light
touches them? One of the most interesting things about John Constable
is that he first made quick sketches of his pictures, then built up his finished
paintings. Many people today think his quick sketches were better
than his finished work!

Art Institute of Chicago

The Herring Net
Winslow Homer (1836–1910) American

Winslow Homer was one of America's greatest painters of fishermen and
the sea. This painting shows two fishermen trying to land a net of fish.
In every line of the painting, we can see the rise and fall of the surging
waves. Do you see how the net rises to a point in the fisherman's hand,
how the silvery fish follow this movement? How many other ways can you
find in which Homer used this pattern to show the surging sea?

Art Exhibits

As MORE and more pictures were painted, more and more people wanted to see them. During the eighteenth century, art galleries and exhibits began to open to help people do this.

Today we have public art museums in many of our cities. We have private art galleries where artists can show their pictures, and people can come and look and buy.

We do not have to go to a palace or a cathedral to see a painting. Often famous paintings travel "on loan" from one museum to another, from the Louvre in Paris to the Art Institute in Chicago, from the Rijks Museum in Amsterdam to the National Gallery in Washington, D.C.

There are many famous paintings in art exhibits. Some are old, and some were painted by artists who are living today. There are paintings, too, that are not yet famous.

We hold art exhibits in other places, too. In summer we often have art fairs in our parks. Sometimes we block off a city street and hold an art fair there. In winter there are art shows in many community houses and town halls.

We have art exhibits in schools, too. Every time you paint a picture in art class and your teacher hangs it on the wall, your picture is on exhibit.

We can have art exhibits in our homes, too, for painting is for everyone. Painting is fun.

Sometimes we give prizes for the best paintings. Sometimes we give no prizes. An art exhibit can be exciting in other ways.

Often we look at things, but we do not really see them. We walk down a street or a country lane, but we do not really see what we pass. Then we may see a painting of that street or road, and we are surprised. Why didn't we notice that clump of trees that looked just like a camel? Why didn't we notice the sleepy stone kitten on the doorstep of that little house?

Next time we walk down that street or road, we will probably look at what we pass. We will find pictures of our own to draw.

41

New Ways of Painting

ARTISTS are always looking at things in a new way. They are always trying new ways of painting. Often these pictures seem strange to people and they laugh at them or perhaps grow angry. But often, too, these pictures are the ones that are remembered best as time goes on.

Many times these pictures lead to a new style, or *school*, of painting. Édouard Manet was one of the great painters who led the way for other painters to follow. His bold and dramatically different use of color made many people angry when they first saw his work. But today we hang his pictures proudly in our museums and art galleries. People are no longer shocked by his style of painting.

The Fifer
Édouard Manet (1832–1883)
French

This is one of the pictures that made the people of Manet's time angry. Do you see how the dull background of the painting contrasts boldly with the bright colors in the fifer's costume? If you were drawing or painting a picture of a fifer or of a bugler in the school band, how would you draw it?

The Louvre, Paris

Jean on a Wooden Horse
Claude Monet (1840–1926) French

Claude Monet liked best to paint landscapes, but sometimes he also painted a
picture of a person. This painting shows his son, Jean. In all his paintings,
Monet tried to show how colors changed in sunlight or shadow. Do you see how
the sun shines on the boy's face and wooden horse and makes them bright?
Do you see how dark the bushes look in the shadows?

One of the great artists who followed Édouard Manet in trying to
find new ways of painting was Claude Monet. He was the leader of a
group of artists called the Impressionists. These artists tried to paint
the feeling, or *impression*, an object gave them. They believed in
painting out-of-doors instead of in studios, because they wanted to
show how colors changed as sunlight changed or when the wind blew
the grass or stirred the water. They wanted to capture the dazzling
colors of nature—the blazing orange of a sunset, the brilliance of a
flowering garden, snow shining in the moonlight or under the sun.   43

Another famous artist who tried a new way of painting was Georges Seurat. He invented a way called Pointillism. He painted tiny dots of blue, green, and yellow, close together, and found that this made a more sparkling, grasslike green than if he had used a ready-mixed green color.

Many people laughed at him when he tried this. But today, when we print color pictures in magazines and books, we use this system of tiny dots of blending colors. One color is printed over another color to make a finished color picture. If you look at the color pictures in this book through a strong magnifying glass, you will see the dots.

This system of dots is also often used in printing black-and-white pictures to deepen shadows and highlight bright areas.

Art Institute of Chicago

La Grande Jatte (Detail)
Georges Seurat (1859–1891) French

Georges Seurat liked to paint people at the circus or on the beach or in the park. La Grande Jatte was an island park in the Seine river near Paris, France, and many people went there for an afternoon of fun. Do you see how the colors sparkle in this painting by Seurat? See, too, how the artist used lines and shapes to create a pattern. Do you make a pattern, too, when you paint a picture?

Backyards, Greenwich Village
John Sloan (1871–1951) American

Before World War I, some American artists wondered why there must
be dirty backyards, tenements, and factories in our cities. They painted
pictures to make others wonder about this, too. People called them
the Ash Can school. Some of their paintings were sad, some were funny,
but always they were painted to make people stop and look and think.
Always these artists tried to give the feeling of the place they painted
more than the way it really looked.

Do you know one thing that has made artists of today try new
ways of painting? It is the camera. Before the camera was invented,
there was only one good way to make a picture of a person, place, or
thing. You had to draw or paint it. Today you can take your camera,
snap the shutter, and get a clear color photograph.

Yet a photograph is not a painting. A painting can be a picture
of a person, place, or thing. But it also has much more in it.

When you type your name, it is just typed letters. It does not tell
that *you* typed it. But when you write your name, it is your hand-
writing. Nobody else in the world writes exactly as you do.

When an artist paints a picture, the same thing happens. Each
artist sees things differently. Each artist uses a brush and paint just
a little differently. Nobody else paints exactly as he paints.

45

Sometimes an artist paints a pattern picture to tell us his ideas. Fernand Léger did that in his painting called *The City*. He did not want to show a real picture of the city. He wanted to share with us his feeling about the city.

Many modern artists do not want to paint a picture of any special thing. Music, say these artists, is sound. It does not imitate the croaking of a frog, the song of a bird, or the swirling of a whirlpool. Painting, say these artists, can be like music. It does not have to imitate the appearance of a frog, a bird, or a whirlpool. It can show only colors, shapes, lines, and surface textures. This kind of painting is called *abstract* painting.

A. E. Gallatin Collection
Philadelphia Museum of Art

The City
Fernand Léger (1881–1955) French

What do you see when you first look at this painting? Is it the harsh color? Is it the stiff, sharp shapes? Is that what the artist wanted us to feel about the city? When you look again, you will see how Léger used the lines of the steps, the shapes of buildings and poles and signs, and the raw, bright colors to form the pattern of his painting. Did you ever try to draw a pattern picture of your own home or school or playground?

Personages with Star
Joan Miró (1893–   ) Spanish

What does this painting say to you? Does it make you feel as if you are looking into a dream world? Do the colors make you feel gay?

We do not know yet whether this new way of painting will live and be remembered or pass and be forgotten. But it is an exciting, new idea—and that is what makes painting an adventure.

When the first cave man took a chunk of red chalk and made a drawing on his rock wall, artists were setting out on a voyage of discovery that led to Michelangelo and his great fresco paintings in St. Peter's cathedral. When Pieter Brueghel painted children playing long ago in Belgium and Holland, artists were setting out on another voyage of discovery that led to the Ash Can school of John Sloan.

There are always new worlds of color and form and composition and design to explore. We can be the explorers. What do you like in a painting? What kind of pictures do you like to paint?

Perhaps you do not like the kind of pictures your friend likes. Perhaps you and he like to paint different kinds of pictures. You and he are friends, but you each see things just a little differently. We each should try to paint a thing as we see it. We each should try to paint in our own special way

47

SCULPTURE

What Is Sculpture?

Like drawing and painting, sculpture is something we can look at and see.

It can be the figure of a man on horseback, sword in hand, ready to charge the enemy. It can be a frisky puppy or a roaring lion or a bucking horse. It can be a carving of a great man we honor and remember like George Washington or Abraham Lincoln. It can be a make-believe modeling of a dragon or a man from Mars.

Sculpture is different from a drawing or a painting. It is solid. If it is a large figure, you can walk around it and see how different it looks from every view. If it is small enough, you can pick it up and turn it about in your hands.

Sculpture is made from clay or bronze or wood or stone or other materials. It has thickness. You can touch it and feel the coolness of the clay, the grain of the wood, the smooth or rough texture of the stone.

But always, like drawing and painting, sculpture shares an idea or expresses how the sculptor feels about things or people he knows or remembers or imagines.

Courtesy of the National Gallery of Art, Index of American Design
White Lady
Colonel Charles A. L. Sampson (?) Bath, Maine

Sculpture can be carved from wood as was this figurehead from the sailing ship "White Lady" of New Bedford, Mass.

Photo Alinari

The Metropolitan Museum of Art,
Gift of Edward S. Harkness, 1917

St. George
Donatello (1386?–1466) Italian

Sculpture can be carved from marble
as was this statue of the
brave knight, St. George.

Hippopotamus
Egyptian (about 1950 B.C.)

It can be modeled from clay like
this little hippopotamus made
long ago in Egypt. How do you
like its design of flowers
and leaves?

Whitney Museum of American Art

Playing Dogs
Hunt Diedrich (1884–1953) American

Sculpture can be cast in bronze as were
these romping dogs.

49

Did you ever try to make clay figures? It is fun to mold the clay and see what kind of forms you can make.

It Is Fun to Model Figures from Clay

Dɪᴅ you ever hold a lump of clay in your hands and wonder what shape was hidden in it? It is like a mystery story. You do not know the answer until the story is done. You can push clay this way and that way. You can squeeze clay and pinch it. And what will you make? Maybe it will look like a dog or a cat. Maybe it will be a figure like no animal or person you ever saw.

You can poke holes in clay and make eyes. You can scratch lines and make a grinning mouth.

Clay is easy to shape while it is moist. You can do exciting things with clay. You can make a shape from one lump of clay, or you can take another lump of clay and push the two lumps together. You can add as many lumps of clay as you need to build your figure.

Clay hardens as it dries, and you can keep your clay figure a long time. You can make the clay still harder by baking, or *firing*, it in the sun or in a special, very hot oven called a *kiln*. Clay that has been fired is called *terra cotta*, or baked earth.

You can paint your clay figure, or you can make it bright and shiny by covering it with melted glass and then baking it in the kiln. This is called giving the clay a *glaze*.

50

Sculptors often cast clay figures in bronze. Does this bronze elephant look like a statue you have seen in a museum or an art gallery?

Sculptors use clay figures as models from which they can make a statue of stone or metal. The clay models must be strong and sturdy so the sculptors make a kind of skeleton of wire and fix it firmly on a clay base. This skeleton is called an *armature*. Then they take lumps of moist clay and cover the skeleton as they build up the figure. When the rough figure is finished, they take tools of wood and wire and make the details, like wrinkles in an elephant's trunk, a lion's mane, or perhaps a boy's hair blowing in the wind.

Then the sculptors take their large clay figures and make a mold and cast them in bronze or in other metals. These figures can last for thousands of years

You can make an armature for a figure and build it up with clay. You can make the details with wooden and wire tools.

51

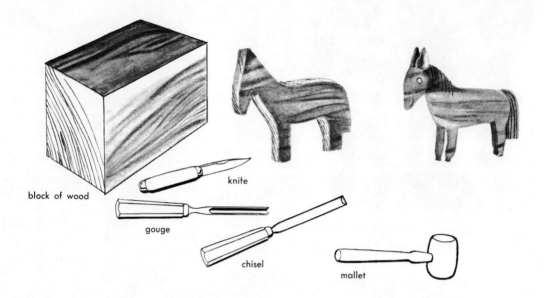

block of wood

knite

gouge

chisel

mallet

It Is Fun to Carve Figures

Wood and stone are not like clay. You cannot twist or squeeze or model them into different shapes. But like a lump of clay, a block of wood or stone or other material holds a shape within it.

Did you ever whittle on a stick of wood? Do you remember how the wood shavings flew away from the strokes of your knife and how pleased you felt as you saw the wood take a shape?

Wood is easy to carve. If it is a soft wood, like white pine, all you need is a sharp knife. If it is a harder wood, like walnut, you need a gouge and a straight-edge chisel, and a mallet with which to hammer.

What shape do you think you can find in the wood? Is it the shape of something you know or remember or imagine? Carve away the wood slowly, stroke by stroke, from top and sides until you see a figure coming out.

When the figure is done, you can smooth away the rough edges. Then you can spread a light coating of shellac over it. You can sand it with a fine-grained sandpaper, and polish it with wax until it has a shiny gloss.

Stone is harder to carve than wood. Sometimes, to help see a form clearly, the sculptor first makes a clay model. Then he works on the block of stone. He roughs out his figure with a pointed chisel and mallet. He uses other chisels to smooth the stone and make the details.

Sculpture Has Many Shapes

THERE are many ways to make shapes of clay or bronze or wood or stone or other materials. Sculpture can be little or big. It can be part of a building or other structure, or it can stand alone. But always it tells us something about what the sculptor feels or thinks about the world he knows.

The Metropolitan Museum of Art, Rogers Fund, 1924

The American Soldier
Jacob Epstein (1880–1959)
American-British

Sculpture can stand alone as this statue does.

Reproduced, by permission of the publisher, The Vanguard Press, from The Art of Ancient Mexico by L. Groth-Kimball and F. Feuchtwanger.

Colossal Head in Basalt, La Venta, Tabasco

Sculpture can be huge. This giant stone head was created by an Olmec sculptor centuries ago in ancient Mexico.

Carving from Notre Dame Cathedral

Sculpture can be part of a building like this make-believe devil carved on the cathedral of Notre Dame in Paris.

Tin, Enameled Earthenware Cow (1700's) Delft, Holland

Sculpture can be as little as this gaily decorated cow that was made long ago in Holland.

Metropolitan Museum of Art, Dick Fund, 1938

Head of David
Michelangelo (1475–1564) Italian

One of our best-loved stories
is that of David, the shepherd
boy who became king.
Hundreds of years ago,
Michelangelo carved a giant
statue of David. Yet as we
look at his head today
it is so alive that we almost
expect David to speak to us.

Photo Alinari

Photo Alinari

Singing Boys
Luca Della Robbia
(1400?–1482) Italian

These singing boys
lived long ago in Florence,
Italy. Do they remind
you of the boys
in your school chorus
or church choir?

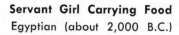

Servant Girl Carrying Food
Egyptian (about 2,000 B.C.)

This carving of a peasant girl
shows how the early Egyptians
carried meats in a basket on their
heads. Do you see the duck in her
hand, too? She was carved from wood
and painted thousands of years
ago. The Egyptians liked to use
straight lines to make their shapes.

54

Metropolitan Museum of Art, N.Y.

Sculpture can be centuries old, and yet we can look at it today. We can touch it and feel its surface beneath our finger tips. Sculpture can be so new that it is still unfinished in the sculptor's studio.

But whether sculpture is old or new, it tells us a story. Sometimes it is the story of how people of other times or other lands lived and worked and played. Sometimes it is a story of today.

Sculpture needs no words to tell us its story. As we look at it, we discover that people of long ago and people of today share many of the same hopes and fears and desires.

Totem Pole
Haidan Indians, Queen Charlotte Islands

This ancient Indian totem pole stands in Lincoln Park, Chicago, Illinois. At its top is a Thunder Bird. The shaft is the body of a Killer-Whale.

The Thinker
Auguste Rodin
(1840–1917) French

The French sculptor Rodin made this statue of *The Thinker*. Although the man is seated, he does not look as if he is at rest. How would you make a statue of somebody thinking?

Metropolitan Museum of Art, Gift of Thomas F. Ryan

55

Courtesy of the Chicago Park District

Detroit Institute of Art

The Frog
John B. Flannagan
(1895–1942) American

The sculptor, John B. Flannagan, carved this frog directly out of field stone. Like ancient sculpture, it keeps the feeling and look of the rock from which it was carved.

Sculpture reflects the time in which it was created. Like a painter, a sculptor shapes figures to express what he sees and knows and remembers and imagines. He shapes figures to express what he feels and thinks.

A sculptor of today does not live in the same way as a sculptor of the Renaissance lived. The figures he creates show this.

Like drawing and painting, sculpture changes as the way we live changes. Sculptors express new ideas in their shapes. They try to use shapes in new ways. They try to use new materials.

Some sculptors today like to make shapes that move. These are called *mobiles*. They make these shapes of wire and sheets of metal and hang them in the air. When the breeze stirs, the shapes move.

Artists know there are many ways to create sculpture. It can be carved from wood or stone or modeled from clay or cast in bronze or other metals. It can be as solid and firm as a rock or it can sway with the blowing breeze.

But always a sculptor creates a shape as he sees or imagines it. Always he expresses what he feels and thinks.

That is what makes sculpture alive and exciting.

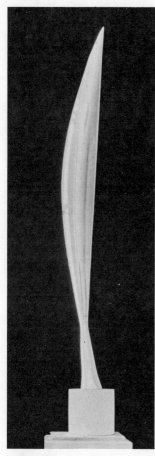

Museum of Modern Art

Bird in Space
Constantin Brancusi
(1876–1957) Rumanian

This sculpture is sometimes
also called *Bird in Flight*.
The sculptor wanted to
suggest the graceful
movement of a bird, not
the way a real bird
looks.

Museum of Modern Art, Gift of Advisory Committee

Lobster Trap and Fish Tail
Alexander Calder (1898–1976) American

A mobile changes its shape with the slightest
movement of the air.

57

Music

Sounds on Parade

THE FOOTBALL stadium is around the corner. We cannot see it yet as we hurry down the street, but we can hear a blare of trumpets and a roll of drums. We break into a run, for we know that the school band is marching out on the football field, and we do not want to miss the parade.

How do we know that the band is marching out?

The trumpets and the drums tell us with their music.

An artist creates a picture with colors and shapes and lines. A sculptor creates shapes of clay or bronze or stone or wood. But how does music tell its story?

We cannot see music, as we can see a painting. We cannot touch music, as we can touch a piece of sculpture. Music tells a story we can hear—a story with sounds.

The band marches out on the football field. "Here we come!" blare the trumpets. ONE, two, three, four! Drums and marching feet beat out the rhythm. ONE, two, three, four! ONE, two, three, four!

We do not have to see the band to know that sounds are on parade.

59

Another street is quiet. The wind rustles the leaves of the trees. On a front porch, a mother hums softly as she rocks her baby to sleep.

A boy on a bicycle whistles gaily. Girls sing as they jump rope.

"Pepper, salt, vinegar," they chant, turning the rope.

The sounds of music are all around us. Each sound is different. Each sound tells its own story.

If we shut our eyes, we will not see the band march out on the football field. We will not see the rustling leaves or the mother humming a lullaby. We will not see the whistling boy or the singing girls.

But we will still hear their music, and we will know if it is exciting or sleepy, gay or sad.

We will know, too, what is making the music.

We will know if it is a trumpet or a drum or some other instrument.

We will know if it is someone humming or whistling or singing.

There are many ways of making music. We can play an instrument or hum or whistle or sing a tune.

We can play and sing alone or with others, but always it is fun to make music.

The Beginning of Music

Do YOU think there was ever a time when there was no music? It is hard to imagine. Sea waves have been breaking against the shores of earth for millions of years. The waves are always moving, and they make high or low sounds. They beat out a rhythm. They make a kind of music.

We can hear this music today, and cave men who lived long, long ago could hear it, too. This is nature's music.

When and how did men begin to make music? Some people think it started with singing. Other people think it started with beating time. We do not know exactly when or how man-made music began.

Perhaps a cave man shouted with pride when he killed a mammoth. Later he shouted again as he told his people of his victory. His shouts made a kind of song. Perhaps he stamped his feet as he shouted his victory song. The beat of his stamping feet made a kind of crude rhythm.

The first musical instruments were probably hands clapping together and feet beating time. Today we still clap our hands to the beat of a song. Our feet still beat time to the exciting rhythm of a march or a dancing tune.

Later a man hollowed out a log and stretched the skin of an animal across it. He beat on this with a stick and that was the first drum.

One day, long ago, a boy watched his sheep beside a river bank. He took a hollow grass stalk and blew through it. Did you ever make a reed whistle? Can you imagine the surprise of that shepherd boy as his notes blew out, high and shrill? Perhaps that was the beginning of our wind instruments.

The ways we make music have changed in many ways since the days of the cave man. But the kinds of music we make are still much the same. Mothers have always sung lullabies. A cave mother had no words or language. She could not sing a tune. But her soft grunts made a sleepy song that a cave baby understood. A baby of today would understand it, too, for always a lullaby is comforting music that makes a baby feel safe and protected and loved.

Children have always made songs to sing as they play. Boys in ancient Egypt sang as they played games beside the river Nile. Girls in long-ago Greece played singing games.

What is the first song you ever sang? Do you remember? Was it a song you sang as you jumped rope or played a game? Did you ever play a game to this song?

Itisket Itasket

Helen Wing

I-tis-ket I-tas-ket, A green and yel-low bas-ket, I

wrote a let-ter to my love and on the way I dropped it, I

dropped it, I dropped it and on the way I dropped it.

This is an action song. The children link hands and form a ring. One child takes a handkerchief and runs around the outside of the ring while the other children circle slowly as they sing. At the last chant of "dropped it," the child who is "It" drops the handkerchief behind someone in the circle and runs on. The other child must pick up the handkerchief and run after "It" and catch him before he reaches the vacant place in the circle. If he does not, he is "It" the next time.

Sur Le Pont D'Avignon
(The Bridge of Avignon)

French Singing Game

Helen Wing

Sur le pont d'A - vi - gnon, L'on y danse, L'on y danse,
On the bridge near the town, Folks are danc-ing, gai-ly danc-ing,

Final Ending

Sur le pont d'A - vi - gnon, L'on y danse tout en rond.
On the bridge near the town, On the bridge of A - vi - gnon.

REFRAIN

Beaux mes-sieurs font comm'- ci, Et puis en - core comm'- ça.
All the lads bow this way, Then a-gain bow that way,

Les belles dames font comm'- ci, Et puis en-core comm' - ça.
Girls all curt-sy this way, Turn and curt-sy that way.

All over the world, children play singing games. Sometimes the games are different from the ones you sing and play. Sometimes your singing games and their singing games are much alike. French children like to play The Bridge of Avignon. Did you ever play a game like it?

The Minstrels

CHILDREN have always played singing games. People have always made music to express what they feel and know and remember and imagine.

In the early days of history, few people could read or write, but they still had stories to tell. Sometimes they drew a picture or carved a statue to tell a story. Many times, they sang their stories. The Vikings of Norway and Denmark were bold sailors and fighters. They sang songs to tell stories of sea battles or of Viking heroes. These story songs traveled from country to country. A sailor from Norway might sing his song in an Irish town. A sailor from Denmark might sing his story in England or France.

The people of France and England and Germany made story songs, too. There were no magazines or newspapers to tell the news in the tenth or eleventh or twelfth centuries. There was no radio or television. But just like you, people wanted to know and tell the things that were happening. They made songs to tell the news.

Traveling musicians, called *minstrels*, sang and played on their harps as they went through the countries. They sang true stories of heroes and battles. They sang sad stories or funny stories. They played and sang in the castles of kings, in village squares and in country inns. They sang stories of their own and stories they had heard others sing. Story songs traveled through many countries.

Folk Songs

THE people liked to listen to the minstrels sing just as you like to listen to records or to songs on radio or on television. But just like you, the people liked to sing, too. Sometimes they sang the songs they had heard the minstrels sing. Many other times, they made up songs of their own. We call these songs *Folk Songs*.

We do not know who first made up these folk songs. We do not know in which country some of these songs were first sung, for some folk songs seem to travel all over the world.

As the songs traveled, they changed, so that often the same song was sung just a little differently in different places and in different times. People loved the songs and sang them and passed them on to their children and their grandchildren. People remembered the songs, but they did not always remember them in exactly the same way. In America today, we sing many folk songs that were first sung in England hundreds of years ago. We do not sing them exactly as the English people of that time sang them. If you hear the song in Maine, it may sound just a little different from the way people sing it in Virginia or Kentucky.

One of these old folk songs is called *Barbara Allen*. Some people sing these words when they sing the song:

> In Scarlet Town where I was bound
> There was a fair maid dwelling,
> Whom I had chosen to be my own,
> And her name was Barbara Allen.

Other people sing these words:

> In Scarlet Town where I was born,
> There was a fair maid dwellin'
> Made every youth cry, "Well-a-day!"
> And her name was Barbara Allen.

There are many other ways to sing this song. Did you ever sing it? What words did you sing?

Sometimes the folk songs of a people reflect their history. During the American Revolution, the British soldiers sang a song to tease the American soldiers. The Americans laughed and began singing the song themselves. When the British surrendered at Yorktown in 1781, the Americans sang that same song. It was "Yankee Doodle."

Yankee Doodle

Helen Wing

Yan-kee Doo-dle went to town A-rid-ing on a po-ny, He stuck a feath-er in his hat and called it mac-a-ro-ni.

Yan-kee Doo-dle keep it up, Yan-kee Doo-dle dan-dy,

Mind the mu-sic and the step and with the girls be han-dy.

Goodbye, Old Paint

Helen Wing

My foot in the stir-rup, my po-ny won't stand, Good-bye, Old Paint, I'm a-leav-in' Chey-enne, I'm a leav-in' Chey-enne, I'm off for Mon-tan'. Good-bye, Old Paint, I'm a leav-in' Chey-enne.

People have always made songs to sing as they marched or played or worked. Cowboys of the old West sang as they rounded up the cattle, or *dogies*. They sang as they watched the herds at night. It kept the cattle quiet and helped time pass swiftly. Do you know this song?

Sailors sang as they raised sail or pulled up anchor. We call these sailing songs *chanteys.* Can you imagine the white sails of the ships billowing in the wind as the sailors sang a song like this?

Blow The Man Down

Helen Wing

Oh, blow the man down, bul-lies, blow the man down, To me way, aye, blow the man down. Blow the man down, bul-lies blow the man down, Give me time to blow the man down.

Erie Canal

Helen Wing

Low bridge, ev-'ry-bod-y down! Low bridge, for we're com-in' to a town! You will al-ways know your neigh-bor And you'll al-ways know your pal, If you've ev-er nav-i-gat-ed on the Er-ie Can-al!

The mule drivers who worked on the Erie Canal sang, too. The canal boats moved slowly, day and night. To keep awake, the mule driver sang about his cargo, announced the time schedule, and told about the work he did. One of his duties was to warn passengers as they came to a low bridge. The song above is one they often sang.

73

The men who laid the railroad tracks also sang as they worked. As they sang, they helped build America, for they laid their tracks across the prairie and the desert. They spanned a vast continent.

The first great railroad chain to stretch from one end of the continent to the other was the Pacific Railroad. The men of the Central Pacific began laying track from Sacramento, California, and worked eastward over the Sierra Nevada Mountains. The men of the Union Pacific began laying track from Omaha, Nebraska, and worked westward toward the Rockies.

The first rail was laid by the Central Pacific on January 8, 1863. For five long years, the men who laid the railroad tracks fought a wilderness. They fought mountains and storms. They fought the Indians, too, for the Sioux and Cheyenne Indians feared and hated the railroad, the Iron Horse that threatened to drive away the buffalo. Yet as the men worked and fought they sang. This is one of the songs they sang.

> I've been working on the railroad,
>   All the livelong day,
> I've been working on the railroad,
>   Just to pass the time away.
>
> Can't you hear the whistle blowing?
>   Rise up so early in the morn,
> Can't you hear the Captain shouting,
>   "Dinah, blow your horn!"

On May 10, 1869, the tracks of the Central Pacific and the Union Pacific met and joined at a place called Promontory Point in the Utah desert north of Great Salt Lake.

Do you wonder that the men sang and cheered?

A golden spike was driven in the last rail to celebrate the great day. A telegram was sent to every part of the nation. This is what the telegraph keys clicked out:

"The last rail is laid . . . the last spike is driven . . . the Pacific Railroad is completed!"

The men who laid the railroad tracks came from many parts of America. They came from other countries, too. Men from China worked for the Central Pacific. Men from Ireland worked for the Union Pacific. They all helped build America.

The songs of our country are part of the history of our country. Like the people of our country, the songs have come from many far lands. They have traveled north, south, east, and west until now they belong to all of us.

The pioneers in the covered wagons fought hostile Indians, hunger, thirst, and disease as they made their way slowly across the great plains to California. But at night they sang beside their lonely campfires. Listen to the gay, lilting music of this old song.

Clementine

Helen Wing

1. In a cav-ern, In a can-yon, ex-ca-vat-ing for a mine, Dwelt a min-er, for-ty nin-er, And his daugh-ter Clem-en-tine.

2. Oh my darl-ing, Oh my darl-ing, Oh my darl-ing Clem-en-tine, Thou art lost and gone for-ev-er, Oh my darl-ing Clem-en-tine.

Later, around 1900, people began collecting these old, old songs and writing them down and putting them in books. They knew that if people stopped singing a song, it would be forgotten. They wanted these songs to be remembered for they help tell the story of the building of our country. They wanted people to keep on singing these songs that are part of our country.

People like Carl Sandburg and John and Alan Lomax and many others traveled from state to state, from county to county, listening to people sing these songs. Sometimes they found a song in a mountain cabin. Sometimes they found a song in a logging camp or in a mining camp or at a rodeo or a country square dance. They wrote down the words and the music of these songs.

Other people, like Burl Ives and John Jacob Niles and Jean Ritchie, and many others, sang these songs and made records of them so we could all hear and learn to sing them, too.

Have you ever heard this song on radio or television? It is an old riddle song. Do you like riddles? Can you guess this one?

I gave my love a cherry that has no stone,
I gave my love a chicken that has no bone,
I gave my love a ring that has no end,
I gave my love a baby with no cryin'.

How can there be a cherry that has no stone?
How can there be a chicken that has no bone?
How can there be a ring that has no end?
How can there be a baby with no cryin'?

A cherry when it's blooming, it has no stone,
A chicken when it's pipping, it has no bone,
A ring when it's rolling, it has no end,
A baby when it's sleeping, there's no cryin'.

Today we often listen to folk songs on records or over radio or television. Some are songs of our own country. Others are folk songs of other lands. As we listen to a song from Africa or France or Spain, we learn a little of how people in those countries live and work and laugh and dream. Did you ever hear Richard Dyer-Bennett or Tom Glazer sing these old English songs?

Hush, Lit'l Baby

Helen Wing

1. Hush, lit'l ba - by don't say a word,
2. If that di - a - mond ring turns brass,

Ma-ma's gon-na buy you a mock-ing bird, If that mock-ing
Ma-ma's gon-na buy you a look-ing glass. If that look-ing

bird don't sing Ma-ma's gon-na buy you a dia-mond ring.
glass gets broke, Ma-ma's gon-na buy you a bil - ly goat.

Composers Write Music

LONG AGO there was no written music. People sang songs they made up or that they had heard other people sing. The songs were passed along from one person to another. Songs changed as different people sang them different ways.

Then a great musical discovery was made. About nine hundred years ago, some Italian monks discovered a way to write a tune, or *melody*. They wrote down the musical sounds, or *notes*, by putting lines and dots together. They were the first writers, or *composers*, of music.

Today composers write many kinds of music. They write music without words. They write music to play and sing. They write music for one person to sing alone or for many persons to sing together.

The first European composers wrote their music only for the church. They wrote songs that a group of church singers could sing together. We call this kind of singing group a *choir*.

Composers today still write music for a choir to sing in church. They write music, too, for a group to sing in a *chorus* in school or on the stage. This kind of music is called *choral* music.

They arrange the music so it will be easy for the different kinds of voices to sing. Girls and women with high voices sing the *soprano* part. Those whose voices are not as high sing the *alto*. Boys and men with high voices sing the *tenor*. Men with very low voices sing the *bass*.

Just as painters mix colors together to get a new color, composers mix musical sounds together to get a new sound. As the soprano and alto, tenor and bass voices sing together, they blend into harmony.

The leader of a chorus or choir helps the singers sing together. He directs them by waving his hands or a stick called a *baton*. He motions when he wants them to sing fast or slow, loud or soft. He helps them express the way he thinks the composer wanted the music to sound.

Did you ever sing in a chorus or a choir? Each section has its own part to sing, but all the sections sing one song together.

Musical Plays

Like painters and sculptors, composers have always tried to find new ways to express what they feel and think and know and remember and imagine.

The first European composers wrote music for people to sing in church. Later they began to write stories set to music. As people acted out the stories, they sang the words instead of speaking them. A musical story or play is called an *opera*.

The first opera was presented in Italy around the year 1600. Soon composers in France and Germany were writing operas, too. People have enjoyed operas for more than three hundred years and composers are still writing them today.

Many operas are famous all over the world. *Aida* is the story of a captive princess in ancient Egypt. The fiery gypsy music and dancing of *Carmen* make our feet tap, and we want to dance, too.

In 1893, Engelbert Humperdinck, a German composer, wrote an opera especially for children. It is based on a fairy tale and is called *Hansel and Gretel.* Did you ever see it?

Another opera for children is called *Amahl and the Night Visitors.* It was written by Gian-Carlo Menotti, and it is a wonderful Christmas story about Amahl, a lame shepherd boy who sees a bright star shining and who receives a visit from the Three Kings, or Wise Men.

It was written for television and was first produced on the Christmas Eve of 1951. The story was made into a book, too, and there are also records of the opera. You can read the book or play the records in your own home or at school. But if you go to an opera, you will know that the best way to enjoy it is to see and hear it acted on the stage.

These children are giving an opera of their own. It tells the story of Poca-
hontas, the brave Indian princess, and how she saved the life of Captain
John Smith. Did you ever try to give an opera of your own? You do not
have to give an opera someone else wrote. You can make up your own
story. You can make up your own words and music to tunes that you know.
It is fun to sing the music and act out the story!

An opera is one kind of play with music. Another kind of musical play is called an *operetta*. Still another kind is called a *musical comedy*. Usually an opera tells a sad story, but an operetta and a musical comedy tell a gay story with music and dancing.

Did you see *South Pacific?* That is a musical comedy. *Babes in Toyland* is an operetta by Victor Herbert. You will find a song from it on the next page.

Do you know the gay, sparkling operettas by Gilbert and Sullivan? Here is one of the duets from *The Mikado*.

KATISHA: There is beauty in the bellow of the blast,
There is grandeur in the growling of the gale,
There is eloquent out-pouring
When the lion is a-roaring,
And the tiger is a-lashing of his tail!

KO-KO: Yes, I like to see a tiger
From the Congo or the Niger,
And especially when lashing of his tail!

KATISHA: Volcanoes have a splendour that is grim,
And earthquakes only terrify the dolts,
But to him who's scientific
There's nothing that's terrific
In the falling of a flight of thunderbolts!
Yes, in spite of all my meekness,
If I have a little weakness,
It's a passion for a flight of thunderbolts.

BOTH: If that is so,
Sing derry down derry!
It's evident, very,
Our tastes are one!
Away we'll go
And merrily marry,
Nor tardily tarry
Till day is done.

Toyland

Glen MacDonough

Victor Herbert

Toy - land! Toy - land! Lit - tle girl and boy - land, While you dwell with - in it ____ You are ev - er hap - py then Child - hood's Joy - land Mys - tic mer - ry Toy - land! Once you pass its bor-ders you can ne'er re-turn a - gain. ____ When gain. ____

The Ballet

AN opera and an operetta and a musical comedy tell a story in a musical play. A story danced to music is called a *ballet*. There is no singing in a ballet, but there is wonderful music. The dancers rise on their toes and leap and spin about the stage to tell the story.

Like the opera, ballet is hundreds of years old. Yet it is always alive because new ballets are being created constantly.

Photo by Anton Bruehl

Sometimes the new ballets are very different from the old ballets. Like painters and sculptors, the people who compose the music for a ballet and the people who create the dances for it are always trying new ways. That is what makes art and music exciting.

A ballet may be a gay story of a rodeo. It may be a sad story or an exciting story or a beautiful fairy tale of a lovely maiden who was changed into a swan. Sometimes it is a Christmas story like "The Nutcracker."

Always a ballet is a story danced to music, a story that needs no words.

Ballet dancers begin training when they are very young. These girls are members of a Children's Ballet Company. Vera Zorina, the dancer on her toes in the photograph above, joined the Ballet Russe de Monte Carlo when she was sixteen.

Wide World Photos

This ballet scene is from "The Nutcracker."

People Make Music Together

Like drawing and painting and sculpture, music has many ways to tell a story. There are many musical ways to express what we feel and think about the things we know and remember and imagine.

But music is different from art. An artist draws or paints his picture. He does it alone. A sculptor makes a shape from clay or wood or stone. He does it alone.

Sometimes a musician composes a song and sings and plays it himself. But many times, people make music together.

A composer writes music. Sometimes it is a song to sing. Sometimes it is a song to play on an instrument. We call the music he writes a musical *composition*.

Usually the composer does not sing or play his own music. Somebody else sings the song. Somebody else plays it.

A composer writes music, but how do we sing or play it? We beat out the rhythm on a drum. We strum a guitar or blow a trumpet or play the piano. We sing the words alone or in a group of singers. We use musical instruments.

Did you ever think of your voice as a musical instrument? Like a violin or a trumpet, it can sing certain kinds of notes best. This is its range.

But even when two different instruments sing the same notes they do not sound alike. You can sing the same notes as a piano, but you will not sound like a piano. A piano can sing the same notes as a cello, but it will not sound like a cello.

Each instrument makes a different sound. Each instrument makes music in its own way.

Photos: American Music Conference

If the trumpeter and the harpist sound the same notes, will their music sound the same?

93

The Instruments That Make Music

W E CAN make music by playing different kinds of instruments.
There are instruments we strike. We call these *percussion* instruments.

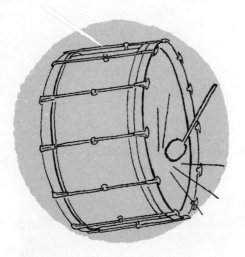

Did you ever play a drum in a
band? One, two, three, four!
It beats out the rhythm.

The big bass drum is also used
in a band. It is used, too,
in a symphony orchestra. It is
the largest of all drums and booms
out loudly.

The kettledrums, or *timpani*, look
like huge brass kettles and are
also used in an orchestra.
The big ones play the low notes.
The small ones play the high notes.

Some of these instruments, like the drums and the cymbals, are among the oldest instruments we know. They were played in ancient times and they are still played today.

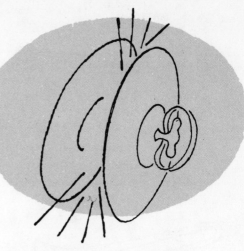

A brass gong is also a percussion instrument. We beat it with a drumstick.

When you hear a loud, crashing sound, it is probably the brass cymbals clashing together in an orchestra or a band.

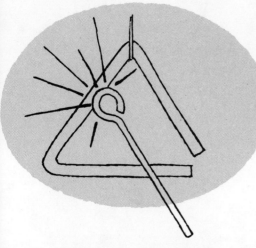

Do you have a triangle in your school band or orchestra? When you strike it with a metal rod, what sound does it make?

We can strike or shake a tambourine. Gypsies often dance to its jingling music. Did you ever dance to a tambourine?

There are many instruments we blow. Some are called the Brass, because they are usually made of brass.

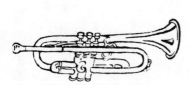

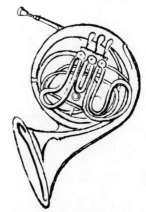

We blow a brass trumpet in a band or an orchestra. It has valves so we can get different tones from it.

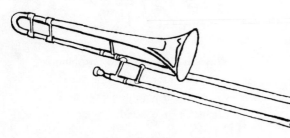

The French horn has a warm, mellow sound. We use it in an orchestra. It blends with both the brass and woodwind instruments.

A brass trombone is blown in a band or an orchestra, too. Part of it slides in and out to make different tones.

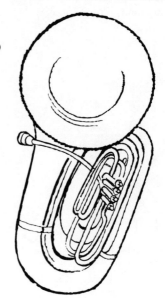

Did you ever blow a bugle? Often we raise or lower the flag to the sound of a bugle.

The tuba is also used in an orchestra. It has a low, very deep tone that adds to the richness of the music. But it can also make scary sounds or funny sounds.

Other instruments we blow are called the Woodwinds.

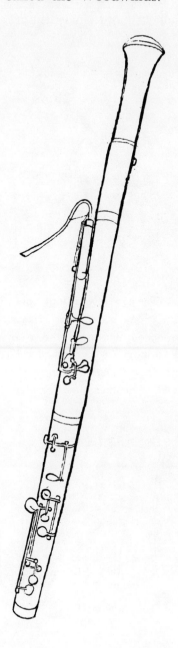

The flute has a high, sweet tone
and is used in an orchestra.
You blow across the mouthpiece
and press the keys with your fingers
to produce different tones.

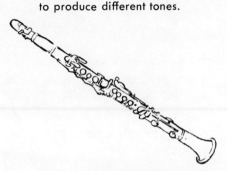

The clarinet is used in an orchestra
and a band. It is made of wood
or metal. Its notes are lower than
a flute's and it has a fuller tone.

The oboe is made of wood
and is a double-reed instrument.
It, too, is used in an orchestra.
Its tone is piercing.

The bassoon is also played in an
orchestra. It is doubled up
to make it easier to play, and
it has a low, deep tone.

Some instruments are called the Strings. We draw a bow across their strings to play them.

A violin has four strings, and we draw a bow across them to play. By moving our fingers up and down on the strings, we can play different notes. A violin can play in an orchestra or in another group or alone.

The viola is much like the violin, but it is bigger. It can play lower notes than the violin, but it cannot play as high notes. It, too, is used in an orchestra or in another musical group.

The cello, or violoncello, is also much like the violin. It is bigger than the viola.

The bass viol is the largest of the String family. The player stands and draws the bow across its strings to produce a deep, rich tone.

Other string instruments are not played with a bow. We pluck them with our fingers or with a *plectrum,* or pick.

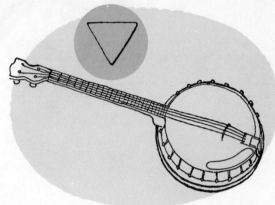

The guitar has a long neck and usually has six strings. We play it by plucking or strumming the strings with our fingers. It is fun to sing to the music of a guitar.

A banjo has a long neck like a guitar, but it has a body like a tam bourine. It usually has five strings, and we play it by plucking its strings with a pick or with our fingers.

A mandolin has a long neck and a pear-shaped body. It has from eight to twelve strings and we pluck it with a pick to play it. Its strings are tuned to the same notes as a violin.

The harp has forty-seven strings, and we play it by plucking the strings with our fingers. It is often used in an orchestra or in other musical groups.

The piano is a wonderful instrument. It is both a string and a percussion instrument. When you strike the piano keys, little hammers make the piano strings move back and forth quickly, or *vibrate*. These vibrations make music.

Some instruments play high notes, and others play low notes. But the piano can play all the notes all the other instruments can play.

You can play a piano at home or in school, in an orchestra or dance band. You can play a piano alone or with somebody else in a duet.

Each instrument makes music in its own way.

A drumskin vibrates when
you beat it.

The air in a trumpet vibrates when
you blow it.

Guitar strings vibrate when
you pluck them.

The strings of a violin vibrate when
you draw a bow across them.

Each instrument makes a different sound. A drum does not sound like a violin. A piano can play the same notes as a trumpet, but it does not sound like a trumpet.

Each instrument sings a song in its own way.

We, too, can make music in our own way. Sometimes there are words to the music. Other times there are no words, only the sounds of music.

We can sing a song or whistle a tune. We can blow a trumpet or beat a drum or play a violin. We can make a song of our own, or we can play music that was written by others.

The music may be gay or sad, but always, through music, we can express a feeling that people everywhere can share and understand.

Often we play music that was written by a composer who lived long ago. As we play we share some of the joy or sadness or hope he expressed through his music.

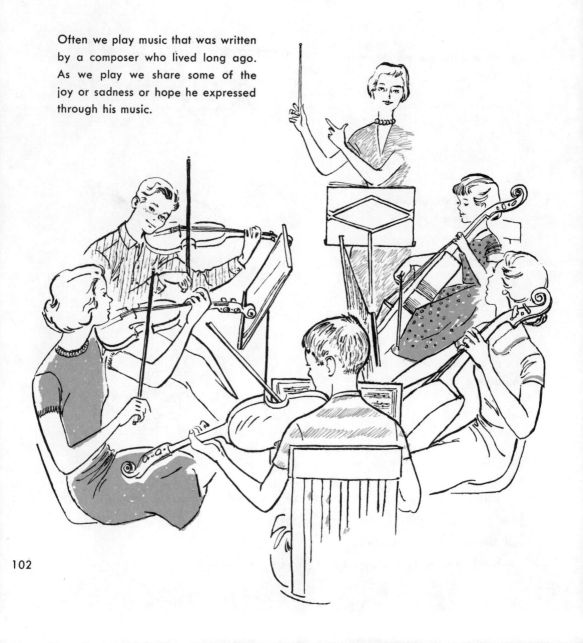

Each instrument can play its own song, but many different kinds of instruments can play together.

Painters can mix different colors together and get a new color. As composers began writing music for instruments to play, they found that they could mix the sounds of different instruments together and create a new sound.

Early in the seventeenth century, composers began writing musical compositions for a small group of instruments to play together.

Usually these instruments were two violins, a viola, and a cello. The composers called this *chamber* music, and we still like to play and listen to this kind of music today.

The Orchestra

THE SEVENTEENTH, eighteenth, and nineteenth centuries were exciting times for music. There were new instruments to play. There were new kinds of music to write for them. Suddenly the air was filled with stirring new musical sounds.

Orchestras began. They grew and grew.

The first orchestras did not sound like our orchestras today. Only string instruments played in them. Usually these instruments were two violins, a viola, and a violoncello.

Then two oboes and two bassoons were added to the orchestra. Later two flutes and two clarinets came in. Now the orchestra had a woodwind section. Composers wrote music for the string instruments and the woodwinds to play together.

Sometimes a pair of trumpets and a pair of kettledrums played with the orchestra. The blare of trumpets and the beat of drums were stirring sounds! That was the beginning of the brass and percussion sections of the orchestra.

Gradually the kettledrums and the trumpets became part of the orchestra. The brass section grew until it had trumpets and horns and trombones and tubas!

Today an orchestra may have a hundred instruments playing in it. But it is still divided into sections of string instruments, woodwinds, brasses, and percussion instruments.

An orchestra has many instruments playing in it. Yet in a way it is one musical instrument.

Does that seem strange to you? If you close your eyes and listen to the string instruments playing, you know that you are hearing violins and violas and cellos. They make a special kind of music. But the music they make does not sound like a whole orchestra.

The woodwinds and brasses and percussion instruments each make their own kind of music. But it is not the music of an orchestra.

All the instruments must play together to make the special kind of music that belongs to an orchestra. That is why we call an orchestra a musical instrument.

Great composers helped orchestras grow and develop.

Franz Josef Haydn, Wolfgang Amadeus Mozart, Ludwig van Beethoven wrote music for new instruments to play. They wrote magnificent music for the new orchestras to play. This kind of music is called a *symphony*.

Today we can hear a symphony at a concert or on a record or over the radio. We can see and hear a symphony orchestra play on television. Sometimes the symphony we hear is new. Many times it is a symphony that was written long ago.

As we listen, we can imagine the surprise and wonder of the people who heard that symphony for the first time long ago when orchestras and symphonies were new.

This is how a symphony orchestra of today looks. It has strings, woodwinds, brasses, and percussion instruments playing together. The leader of an orchestra is called a conductor. He waves his baton to guide the musicians and help them play the music as he thinks the composer wanted it played.

Can you imagine how a composer feels the first time he hears an orchestra play a symphony he has written? Do you think he feels happy and thrilled? Do you know that perhaps he may feel a little surprised, too?

A composer can write a symphony, but he cannot play it himself. A symphony is played by an orchestra made up of many instruments. The composer cannot know exactly how his symphony will sound until he hears it played by an orchestra.

He knows how each instrument sounds alone. He can write notes for a flute to play, high and sweet. He can write notes for a tuba to rumble, low and deep. He can mix the music of many instruments to tell what he feels and thinks about things he knows and remembers and imagines.

There are usually three or four sections, or *movements*, in a symphony. The composer can give each movement a name to tell the musicians and the orchestra conductor how he wants his music played.

He may call the first movement *allegro*, so they will play it in a gay, lively way.

He may name the second movement *andante*, so they will play it slowly and quietly and with a singing quality.

He may call the third movement a *minuet*, so they will play it with a dancing rhythm.

Usually he will call the last movement the *finale*, which means the end. Often this movement is played gaily and fast.

But even though the composer writes the notes and marks the beat and rhythm and names the movements, he still cannot know exactly how the symphony will sound.

For music is like painting. No two artists paint the same object in exactly the same way. No two musicians play the same music in exactly the same way. No two conductors interpret a symphony in exactly the same way. That is why listening to a symphony is always an adventure. A symphony may be hundreds of years old, but each time it is played it sounds different.

The next time you hear a symphony, listen carefully. The conductor and the musicians are trying to tell you just what the composer thought and felt—all in the wonderful language of music.

The famous Greek conductor Dimitri Mitropoulos was also noted as a pianist and a composer. Here he is conducting a rehearsal of the string section of the New York Philharmonic Orchestra. The first violins are toward the front. The second violins and the violas are toward the back. Do you see how he is signaling to the string instruments?

As more and more people listened to music and as more and more people made music, music changed and changed. For music, like art, changes as the way people live changes. It changes, too, as new composers write music. Each composer sees and thinks and feels just a little differently from another composer. The music he writes reflects this.

Composers use old rhythms and tunes to make new rhythms and melodies. They try new beats and rhythms. They find new things to say in new ways.

OH, SUSANNA

I come from Alabama
   With my banjo on my knee,
I'm going to Louisiana,
   My Susanna for to see.

chorus
Oh, Susanna!
   Oh don't you cry for me,
For I come from Alabama
   With my banjo on my knee.

But while composers try to use sounds and rhythms in new ways, they also know and love and remember the music that people have sung and played for many years.

Sometimes they weave the old songs into their new musical compositions. The American composer Roy Harris loved old folk songs, and he used so many in his *Fourth Symphony* that people often call it the *Folk Song Symphony*.

Other composers try to write songs that are like the old folk songs. Stephen Foster did this so well that his songs have become part of the heritage of our country.

Do you know "Oh, Susanna" by Stephen Foster? Does it remind you of a folk song you know and sing or play?

Music, the Universal Language

Long ago people danced to the music of the minuet. Later they danced to the waltz. How surprised and shocked some people were when the waltz was first introduced! It was new, so many people did not like it.

Today the waltz is an old dance to us, but we still dance to its music. We dance to the syncopated beat of a jazz band. We dance to the South American rhythm of a tango or a rhumba.

We are not afraid to try new ways, for our world has grown wider. We can turn a radio knob and hear music from Germany or France. We can turn a television knob and see people dancing in Africa or Peru. The music and dancing may seem strange to us, but as we listen and watch, we grow to understand that all people sing and dance and make music to express the same kinds of feelings.

We sing when we are happy or sad. We dance to music when we are gay. The beat and rhythm of the music may be different, but the spirit and feeling are the same.

Music is alive and exciting as art is alive and exciting because the artists who create music and art are always searching for and finding new ways to say old things.

Long ago in the jungle, people danced to the booming of drums and the rattling of gourds. When the Negroes came to America, they brought this music with them and made it part of American life.

The beat and rhythm of Dixieland today may be different from the booming of the jungle drums, but much of the feeling it creates is the same. As we listen to it, we share some of the excitement those jungle people felt long ago.

Dixieland and swing, ragtime and rock-and-roll, and many other forms of jazz music remind us that music is always old and always new. Always the beat and rhythm call to us and we answer.

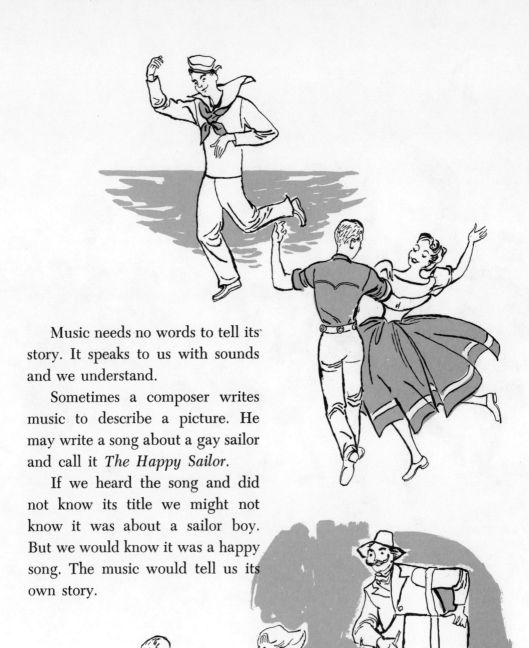

Music needs no words to tell its story. It speaks to us with sounds and we understand.

Sometimes a composer writes music to describe a picture. He may write a song about a gay sailor and call it *The Happy Sailor.*

If we heard the song and did not know its title we might not know it was about a sailor boy. But we would know it was a happy song. The music would tell us its own story.

The sounds of music are all around us. Each speaks to us in its own way. Each of us, too, makes music in his own way.

But always music expresses a feeling that people of all lands can understand and share. Always it sings and plays about hopes and fears and dreams that belong to all people everywhere.

Music is a universal language.

Drama

Play and Pantomime

ONE Saturday afternoon in September a boy ran across an empty lot next door to his home. His arm was bent as though he hugged a ball against his chest. He dashed straight across an invisible line.

"Touchdown!" he yelled proudly.

Can you guess what the boy was doing? He was pretending he was a football hero. How do we know? Like an actor on a stage, he acted out his story and told us so.

An artist draws or paints a picture to tell a story. A musician tells a story with musical sounds. How does an actor tell a story?

He has many ways. Sometimes he tells a story without words. Then his actions alone tell us what he is doing and thinking and feeling

Sometimes he uses words and actions to tell a story.

Sometimes he acts alone. Sometimes he acts with other actors.

But always, like an artist and a musician, an actor tells a story to express what he knows and feels and imagines.

Does an actor on a stage seem far away and strange to you? Did you ever act in a play at school or in church or perhaps in your own back yard? Then you are an actor, too!

But we do not always act out our stories on a stage. Sometimes, like the boy who acted out his football story, we act out stories when we are alone. They are make-believe stories about things we would like to do or people we would like to be.

Did you ever make believe you were a football hero or a girl cheer leader? Boys and girls have always liked to play *let's pretend*. You can pretend to be anyone you'd like to be.

It is like having two worlds. One is the real world. The other is the wonderful world of the imagination. In that world, for a little while, you can go anywhere you want to go, do anything you want to do, be anyone you want to be.

A little boy can be a bear growling in his cave under a table.

A little girl can be a grown-up lady in her mother's high-heeled shoes and best hat.

A boy can be a cowboy of the old Wild West or a deep-sea diver searching for a buried treasure ship.

A girl can be a ballet dancer or a brave nurse on the battlefield or a princess on a golden throne.

When you act out a story by yourself, without words, it is called *pantomime*.

Pantomime Every Day

YOU use bits of pantomime every day. You smile to show you are happy or pleased or proud. You frown to show you are sad or cross or puzzled.

You wave your hand to say "Hello!" to a friend across the street. You put your finger to your lips to motion, "Hush! Be quiet!"

You nod your head to say "Yes" and shake it to say "No" in pantomime.

You walk slowly when you are going to the dentist. You walk gaily when you are going to a Halloween party.

The actions of your face and head and body show what you are feeling and thinking.

117

People have always used pantomine. Long ago when men first began to talk, they knew only a few words. They used the movements of their hands and bodies to act out what they wanted to say.

And when Christopher Columbus discovered America, he used sign language, too, to talk to the Indians he found here. Just imagine the three little ships, the *Nina,* the *Pinta,* and the *Santa Maria,* sailing up to the strange, new land. Admiral Columbus and his brave captains rowed to the sandy beach. Indians crowded through the trees to stare at these strangers who had come from the sea.

Christopher Columbus and the Indians could not talk to each other in words, but they could use actions to say, "I am a friend."

Today if you traveled in a foreign land and did not know its language, you would probably use sign talk, too, to act out what you wanted to say. And people in Mexico or France, Greenland or India or Africa, would understand if you showed them in signs that you were hungry or thirsty, happy or sad.

For people all over the world and in every time have had much the same feelings and have shown them in much the same ways.

If you had no words to say
you were thirsty
how could you ask for a drink?

You and Pantomime

ALL PEOPLE use pantomime to tell what they feel and think. But no two people smile or walk or sit or move in exactly the same way. The way you move tells much about you.

It tells how old you are. You and your baby brother and your grandfather do not move in the same way.

It tells how you feel. You move differently when you are tired or excited or waiting impatiently for the school bell to ring so you can go to baseball practice.

It tells something, too, about the kind of person you are. Are you always in a hurry? Are you the kind of person who likes to do things slowly and carefully? Your actions help show this.

What do you like to do best? Are you a star baseball player? Are you better, perhaps, at making things with your hands? Each person is good at doing different kinds of things, and the way he moves shows this, too.

Your actions also tell something about the kind of person you are deep inside. You smile when you are happy. But do you smile, too, when you are tired or discouraged or afraid? In pantomime you show something of the way you feel and think and are.

A baby just learning to walk, a boy, and an old man
with a cane move in different ways.
What does the way they move tell about them?

Can you guess what the boy
in this picture is pretending?
What bits of pantomime
show it?

Plays in Pantomime

WE use pantomime in our everyday lives. We use it, too, when we act out a pretend story.

Sometimes we play *let's pretend* alone. Other times we play a pantomime game. Did you ever try that? You act out a pantomime and your friends try to guess who you are pretending to be.

Sometimes we act out a pantomime for a program in school or in church. Did you ever act out the story of Paul Revere's Ride or Washington crossing the Delaware?

What story are the boys
and girls in this picture
acting out? How do they
show it?

People have been acting out stories in pantomime for thousands of years. Long, long ago, early men danced about a campfire to act out the story of a hunt. Some wore the skins of wild animals and pretended they were the hunted animals. Others played the hunters. This was the way primitive man asked his gods for a good hunt.

The early Greeks used pantomime, too, as they danced and sang in honor of their god Dionysus. They acted out their thanks to him for a good harvest.

We still use pantomime in our churches today as we act out the Christmas story. But we use pantomime, too, to act out a story on the stage and in the movies and on television.

Clowns in the circus use pantomime to act out a story. Often they use no words at all, but we laugh and laugh because their actions are so funny. We do not need words to tell us what they are doing and why they are doing it.

Actors use pantomime in plays on the stage and in the movies and on television. The next time you go to a movie or watch a television show, notice how the actors move. What do they do to show what they are feeling and thinking? How do they act to show what kind of story people they are pretending to be?

Often when you watch a television play, the camera moves in close to the actor. All you can see is the actor's face. No word is spoken, but you know what the actor is feeling and thinking. The actions of his face tell you.

Actors use words as well as pantomime when they act out a story. But can you imagine a play that had only words, no action or pantomime at all? What would you see? Would it be like this?

What are the actors in this picture doing? How much of the story do they tell you? Are they making the story seem alive and real? Would you want to watch a play that was all like this?

You can see why you need pantomime to act out a story and make it seem alive and real.

You can act out a *let's pretend* story in pantomime when you are alone. As you act it out, for a little while you can be anybody you want to be.

You can act out a story in pantomime at home or at school or in the circus or on a stage. Your actions will tell what the story is about.

But pantomime is only one way to act out a story.

When you go to the movies or watch a story on television or go to the theater, usually you see a story acted out in another way.

Usually the story is acted out with words and pantomime in a play, or *drama*.

What are the actors in this picture doing? Does it make the story seem more alive and real? Why?

123

A Make-Believe World

IT IS exciting to see a play. The lights in the theater go out. The lights on the stage go on. And up there is a little, make-believe world where we can see and hear a story come alive. The story people laugh or cry, and we want to laugh or cry with them. The story people sail off on a ship searching for Treasure Island, and, as we watch, we are sailing on that ship, too.

We share their adventures. We shiver with delighted excitement when young Jim Hawkins meets wily Long John Silver.

Young Jim is our friend. We cower with him in the apple barrel as he listens to the pirates plotting. What will happen next? Will the wicked pirates be able to steal away the treasure?

Did you ever read the story of *Treasure Island*? Did you ever see it acted on the stage or in a movie? Did you ever act in it yourself?

Robert Louis Stevenson wrote the book *Treasure Island* a long time ago. Today we still read the story. We still watch it acted on the stage. And as we watch, the story comes alive for us. Once again that brave little crew sails off to search for buried treasure, and we sail with them.

A play is better than a magic carpet. It is better than a jet plane or a rocket. It can take us to a world of long ago when pirates flew the Jolly Roger. It can take us to a world of the future when men travel to the stars.

It can take us to faraway lands or it can take us to a world that is just like our own street and town.

Sometimes a play is a tale of adventure and daring and courage. Sometimes it is a mystery story. Sometimes it is a story that makes us laugh. Sometimes it is a story that makes us want to cry with the story people.

That is the magic of the make-believe world of a play. It can take us into another world, and while we watch that world is real for us. The story people are real, and we share their hopes and their fears and their courage.

125

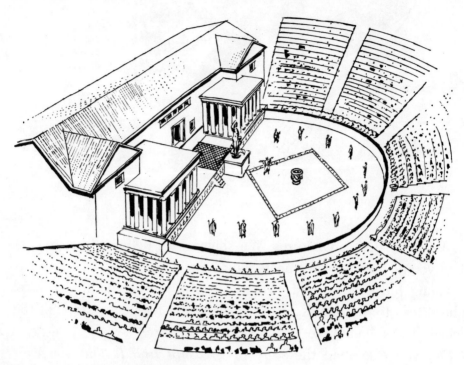

The Story of Thespis

A PANTOMIME tells a story through action. A play tells a story with pantomime and spoken words. The actors talk to each other as they act out the story. This is called *dialogue*.

Did you ever wonder when the first play was acted? It happened centuries ago in Greece. Long before Christ was born, the ancient Greeks sang and danced as they acted out a story in praise of their god Dionysus. But no words were spoken.

Then, so the legend goes, a poet, called Thespis, acted the part of the god. When the people sang and danced, he spoke to them. They sang back their answers to him. This was the first time that dialogue was used in a play.

It was a new idea then. Some people did not like it because it was new and strange to them. But many other people liked it very much. Ever since then actors have talked to each other to help act out the story of a play.

We do not know how much of the legend of Thespis is true. But even today, actors are sometimes called *thespians*.

The picture above is of a play being given in ancient Greece. Does the Greek theater look different from the ones we have today?

BETH (at telephone): Mary, I'm sorry,
but I can't go to the movies with
you tonight. I have to stay home
and baby-sit with my little brother.

How would you act this out in a play?
Did you notice how the stage direc-
tions and dialogue are printed under
this picture? That is the way they are
printed in a play script.

Dialogue Tells a Story

NEXT TIME you watch a television play, listen to the dialogue.
What do the words tell you about
the story?

You use words every day to tell
what you are doing and why you
are doing it. Suppose you plan to
go to a movie with a friend. Then
you find you have to stay home and
baby-sit with your little brother.
What do you do? Probably you
call your friend and tell her.

In a play, dialogue is used in
much the same way, but there is
an important difference.

When you stay home, probably nothing exciting happens. It is
different in a play. Something exciting will happen just *because* the
girl in the play has to stay home. That is why the girl's conversation
with her friend is in the play. It is there to tell the story.

Dialogue also tells about the story people, or *characters*, in a play.
Each character talks in his own way. What he says and how he says
it tell many things about him.

Like a character in a play, each person talks in his own way. Can you imagine how
each of these boys and girls would talk? What dialogue would you write for each?

Dialogue tells many things about the characters in a play.

It tells who each character is, for just like people, each character is different from another character. You and your best friend do not talk in exactly the same way because you do not think or feel in exactly the same way. The way you talk shows this. The way each character in a play talks shows this, too.

Dialogue tells how old a character in a play is. A boy and an old woman and a baby girl will all talk differently.

It tells where the character lives. A boy from Texas does not sound exactly like a boy from Maine. A girl from Iowa does not sound just like a girl from Georgia. Their voices are different, and some of the words they use are just a little different, too.

Dialogue tells at what time the character is living. If the play is about a story that could be happening today, then the characters will talk much as we do.

But if the play is happening in the times of Robin Hood or King Arthur or the American Revolution, then the characters in it will talk as the people who lived then talked.

Robin Hood will not talk like a boy of King Arthur's court. He will not talk as a soldier in George Washington's army talked. He will not talk as we do today.

Dialogue tells us another thing about the characters in a play. It tells us something about the way they live.

King Arthur will not talk like one of his poor woodcutters. A fisherman will use different words than a scientist. A pirate and a jet pilot and a cowboy will all talk in different ways.

Dialogue tells us another important thing. It tells us how the characters are related to each other.

You speak one way when you talk to your teacher. You speak another way when you talk to your father or mother. You speak still another way when you talk to your friends. The words you use are a little different and the way you say them is different, too.

The characters in a play use dialogue in this way, too.

Just for fun, try to write a play of your own. Can you imagine how the characters in it will talk? What will they say to tell about themselves and the play story?

Your voice can sound thin or deep. It can be a whisper when you are frightened.

Dialogue tells the story of the play through words. The way the characters speak the words also helps tell the play story.

If you are reciting and know your lesson, you speak easily. If you do not know your lesson, you stop and hesitate and stumble over words. An actor in a play does this, too, when he wants to show that a character is worried or unsure of what he is saying.

You speak quickly and jerkily if you are excited or angry. You speak slowly if you are tired. The way you talk tells what is happening and what you think and feel about it.

Voices change as feelings change. Listen to the voices around you. Even if you could not hear the words, the sounds of the voices would tell you if they were angry or sad or happy.

Your voice can sound high or low. It can be a shout when you are excited.

A Play Tells a Story

IN A PLAY, the actors use their voices to tell us what the story characters are thinking and feeling. They speak the dialogue quickly or slowly, loudly or softly. They make their voices sound gay or sad, gentle or stern, courageous or afraid.

As they talk to each other, they act out the story in pantomime. The play comes alive for us, and we share the story adventures.

Do you know that we, too, do something as we watch the play? We are the audience. We help make the play come alive for the actors on the stage!

It is fun to act out a story for yourself when no one is there to see. But it is even more fun to act out a story when people are watching and sharing the excitement with you.

It is still more fun when people who are watching you act out the play understand how you are doing it.

Let's pretend we are going to see a play. What kind of play would you like to see? There are many kinds of plays, funny or sad, filled with adventure or mystery. There are plays about here and now and, plays about lands far away and long ago.

Every play tells a story.

Did you ever think about a story? What makes a story?

Suppose there is a storm and a shipwreck. That is exciting to watch. But is it a story? A story must have more than exciting action. It must have characters to whom the action *happens.* The characters in a story should make us care very much about what is happening to them.

Suppose we see a boy all alone on that ship. We will wonder why he is alone. We will wonder what will happen to him. What will he do? How can he fight the stormy seas? How can we help him to safety?

That is the story.

Every play has to have some kind of fight or struggle in it. This is called *conflict.* There are many kinds of conflict.

There is conflict between people and nature—like the boy's fight against the stormy seas.

We are the audience. We help make the play come alive.

There is conflict between people who have different ideas. The story of Christopher Columbus tells about conflict like that.

Columbus believed the world was round. Many people laughed at him. They believed that the world was flat and that a ship could sail over the edge of the world and drop off!

Columbus had to fight the ideas of these men so he could get ships and sailors to sail with him on his voyage. He won his fight, and he discovered America.

You can see why it would be exciting to watch a play about brave Christopher Columbus!

This boy and dog are having fun, but the boy knows that the dog does not belong to him. Can you be happy for long when you know you are doing wrong? Do you think you would like to watch a play about a conflict like this?

Sometimes a play is about a struggle, or conflict, inside one person. At times we all want to do things that we know are wrong. Then we have to fight ourselves to do the right thing.

Suppose the play is about a boy who wants a dog very much. One day he finds a little, lost dog who is wearing a collar. On the collar is the name of the dog's owner. The boy knows he should return the dog to its real master. But he likes the dog, and the dog likes him. What will he do? Will he keep the dog? That is the story—the story of a struggle inside one person to do the right thing.

There are many plays about this kind of conflict. There are many plays, too, about another kind of conflict—the struggle between two people who want the same thing.

Suppose the play is about two boys who each want to be football captain. Which boy will win? How will he win? That is the story.

This kind of conflict play does not have to be a sports story. It can be an adventure story or a love story or a mystery story or a space story. It can be any kind of story in which two people fight for the same thing. Always one person will win, and the other will lose. That will be the story.

Mystery and detective plays have another kind of conflict. A man breaks the law, and the police and detectives try to catch him. You can see many plays like this on television and in the movies.

Conflict can be funny, too. Do you like to watch the little animal cartoons in the movies or on television?

Sometimes a big cat tries to catch a tiny mouse, but the mouse makes fun of him and always gets away.

Sometimes a little canary teases a big cat. It always gets away, too, and we laugh and laugh. Do you know one reason we like to watch stories like this? We like to see the little hero win the conflict over the big giant cat!

The next time you watch a funny play, try and see what kind of story conflict it tells about. For every play, sad or funny, has conflict in it. It is the conflict that makes the play exciting.

Does this remind you of a cartoon you saw in the movies? Did you laugh at the cat and mouse?

A Play Has a Setting

EVERY play has to have a story conflict. What else does a play need? Every play must have a place and a time where and when the action of the story happens. We call this the *setting*.

How does a play show this? It tells it through the dialogue of the characters in the play. Often, too, it shows it by the way the stage looks.

The stage can show an inside scene like a living room or a kitchen or a castle hall. It can show an outdoor scene like a ranch corral or a mountainside or a sandy beach. These are called the *stage sets* or *scenery*.

There can be pictures on the walls and chairs and tables and other furniture on the stage. There can be cookies and lemonade and other foods or drinks on the tables. Sometimes these are real and sometimes they are only pretend. But all these things help make the play seem real. They are called the *stage properties*.

Always the scenery and the stage properties show us when and where the story of a play is happening.

A castle hall of long ago would look very different from your living room today. How many things can you see in this picture that show this?

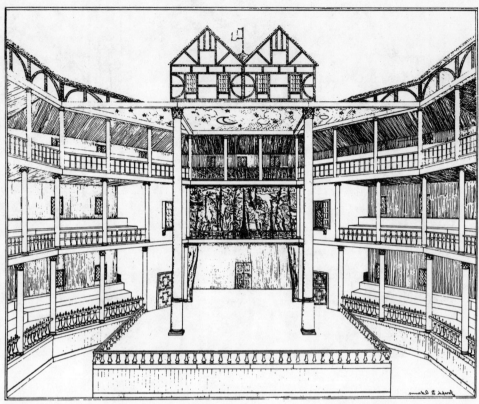

The Folger Shakespeare Library Prints

This is the way the stage of the Globe Playhouse looked when
Shakespeare was alive and his plays were acted on it.

You do not always have to use scenery and stage properties to show
where and when a play is happening. Sometimes the audience can
just imagine the setting.

In the days when William Shakespeare was alive, little scenery was
used. The plays were given in an open court. The stage was a platform
set out from one wall. Sometimes there were curtains with scenes
painted on them to show the setting. Often a simple sign was hung
on the stage. *The Forest of Arden*, it might say.

The noblemen sat in the covered galleries around the stage. The
common people stood in the open pit and looked up at the stage. To
all of them, the stage was a thick forest of tall, green trees. That was
how they imagined it.

Scenery and stage properties make a stage scene seem real. But
it is fun to use our imaginations, too.

135

The Beginning of English Plays

PEOPLE have been giving plays for thousands of years. They have used many kinds of stage settings.

The first English plays were given inside the churches. During the tenth century, only Latin was spoken in the church services. Few country people understood Latin. They could not understand what the priests were saying. How could the priests teach the people the wonderful stories of the Bible?

The priests had an idea. They made up little plays from the Bible stories and acted them out for the people. These plays are called Miracle Plays. The people did not have to understand the words to understand the action of the plays. Just as we do today, the priests acted out the Easter story and the Christmas story and other Bible stories. The people liked the plays and many came to see them.

Soon the churches could not hold all the people. Then the priests acted out the plays on the church porches or in the churchyards.

When the plays moved outside the churches, they changed. They still told Bible stories, but the actors spoke English, not Latin. The characters in the plays began to sound like real people.

The priests stopped acting in the plays. Carpenters, merchants, and other kinds of working people formed their own acting companies. Each kind of worker had his own society, or *guild*. Each guild gave its own special play. For instance, the shipbuilder's guild acted out the story of the building of Noah's Ark.

Often these guild actors gave their plays on a large wagon called a *pageant*. They moved this pageant from place to place and acted the play over and over so all the people in the town could see it. Later people began calling the play itself a pageant.

Today we have pageants of many kinds. A parade of floats on a holiday is one kind of pageant. An outdoor play given to celebrate a special day in history is another kind of pageant.

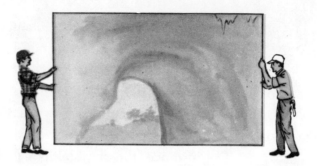

Stage settings have changed in many ways since the days when guilds acted plays on wagons called pageants. Like painters and musicians, stage designers who create stage settings are always trying new ways and new ideas. But they keep many old ideas, too.

Actors do not act on wagons that roll from one place to another now. But there are stage sets that roll on and off a stage. There are stages that turn round and round.

During the Renaissance, great Italian painters like Raphael and Leonardo da Vinci were learning to use perspective in their paintings to show scenes that looked near or far away. Italian artists used perspective in painting stage scenery, too. Artists today also use perspective to make stage scenes look near or far away.

In the nineteenth century, people began using gas instead of candles or oil lamps to light the stage. Today we use electricity to make parts of the stage dark or bright. We use lights of different colors to create moonlight or sunlight, a happy scene or a sad scene or an eery scene like that of the witches in *Macbeth*.

Can you imagine the three witches saying: "Double, double toil and trouble;
Fire, burn; and, caldron, bubble."

A stage setting can seem so real that you almost feel that you can climb a stage mountain or swim in a stage sea. When you go to the movies, often the stage setting you see is real. A cowboy picture is often acted on a real ranch. A sea picture is often acted on a real ship on the ocean.

But a stage setting does not have to be real. It is fun to watch a play in a theater and see the wonderful scenery and stage properties. But it is even more fun to make your own scenery and properties when you give a play at school or at home.

You can paint a mountain scene with crayons or water colors. You can make a cardboard moon or cover a box with brown wrapping paper to make a rock. You can use orange crates and cardboard boxes for chairs and tables and other stage furniture.

And just like the scenery in a theater or in a movie or television play, your stage setting will show where and when the action of the play is happening.

It will help create a little make-believe world where the story of the play comes alive.

139

The Graham Children   Tate Gallery, London

William Hogarth (1697–1764) British

The artist who painted this picture lived and worked in the eighteenth
century. What does the way the children in the painting are dressed tell
you about them? What does it tell you about the way they lived?

Costumes Tell a Story

I**T IS FUN** to dress up when you act out a *let's pretend* story. Actors in a play wear costumes, too, and the costumes help tell the story of the play.

How do they help tell the story? Like the stage setting, costumes show where and when the action of the play is happening.

Suppose the curtain goes up in a theater, and on the stage you see a Pilgrim girl at a spinning wheel. An Indian is standing in the doorway, watching her.

What does that tell you about the play? You will not need words to know that the play is about America in the days of the Pilgrims.

The spinning wheel helped show you that. It is a stage property. The costumes the girl and the Indian wear also show you that. They help tell you where and when the story of the play is happening.

Costumes show you where and when the action of the play is taking place. They also tell you something about the characters in the play.

They show you who the characters are. The captain of a ship dresses differently from a cabin boy. A queen dresses differently from a goose girl. A policeman and a doctor and a fireman all wear different kinds of clothes.

The costumes tell you, too, something about how the story characters think and feel.

Suppose there are two girls on the stage dressed in shabby clothes. One girl is ragged. Her hair is uncombed and her face is dirty. The other girl has patched her clothes neatly. Her hair is tidy and her face is clean. What do their costumes tell you about the girls themselves? How are they different?

142

Did you ever make your own costumes when you gave a play at home or at school? It is fun to do. Gold paper makes a shiny crown for a king or a queen. A red bandanna and a black paper patch can make you look like a fierce pirate. An old fur rug can turn you into a bear or a wolf or a tiger!

All you need is imagination—and some paper and paste and pins and cheesecloth and some old clothes your mother will let you use.

Sometimes it is exciting, too, to give a play and use no costumes at all.

This is harder to do. But you can pretend you are a pirate and walk like a pirate and talk like a pirate and feel like a pirate. And if you do it well enough, the audience will know you are a pirate! You and the audience will be in that wonderful world of imagination where a play comes alive.

143

His make-up and costume make this actor look like a clown.
But he has to act like a clown, too, to make us laugh.

Make-up and Masks

IN THE make-believe world of a play anything can happen. You can pretend to be anyone you want to be. You can act it out with dialogue and pantomime. You can put on a costume and pretend to be George Washington or Tom Sawyer or Long John Silver.

You can even change your face!

An actor changes his face many times for he often plays many different kinds of characters.

With grease paint, an actor can add lines to his face to make it look young or old, kind or wicked. He can add bushy eyebrows and a ragged beard to look like Robinson Crusoe. He can do many other things to change his face with make-up.

An actor can have many kinds of faces with make-up, but make-up alone will not tell the story for him. He has to use pantomime, too, to act out the story. He has to walk differently and talk differently and feel and think differently to make an audience believe he is the character he is playing.

144

People have always tried to change the appearance of their faces as they acted out a story or a play. Long ago ancient man wore the head of an animal as he acted out a hunting story.

The Iroquois Indians of North America wore strange False Face masks as they shook rattles and danced to drive away evil spirits. Today we are not afraid of evil spirits, but we wear scary or funny masks on Halloween.

Three thousand years ago when Greek actors gave a play, they wore masks to show the character they were playing.

Only boys and men could act in a Greek play. Girls and women were not allowed on the stage. The boys and men had to take all the parts so they wore a mask to show if they were playing a boy or girl, a man or woman. The masks also showed what the characters were feeling. There were smiling masks to show joy and frowning masks to show anger and many other kinds of masks.

There were masks, too, to show if the play was a funny play, or *comedy*, or a sad play, or *tragedy*. We still use the words comedy or tragedy today. We still use the Greek masks of comedy and tragedy as signs, or symbols, of plays and acting and the theater.

People all over the world have used masks as they acted out a story. We have fun with masks on Halloween today, too.

You Can Give a Play

IT IS exciting to watch a play, but it is even more exciting to give a play of your own. You can give any kind of play you choose.

You can act out a story alone, or you can act out a story with other people in dialogue and pantomime.

You can make up a story and act it out. It can be a sport story or a mystery, a funny story or a sad story. It can be a story about anything you know or think or feel or imagine.

You can make up your own story, or, if you choose, you can act out a story from a favorite book. If you like, you can take only one part of the story and make a play about it.

But perhaps you want to tell the whole story of the book in a play. How can you do that? You cannot act out every little thing that happened because it would take too long. But you can decide what parts of the book you will need to tell the story clearly. That will be your story play.

It is fun to make a play out of a story book. It is fun to act out your favorite story characters like Tom Sawyer or Mary Poppins or others. Did you ever try it?

Another way to make a play is to act out a story that really did happen. Often in school, you act out a history story to celebrate a holiday. Maybe you give a play about the Pilgrims and the first Thanksgiving. On Columbus Day, you may give a play about the discovery of America. It is always exciting to make history come alive in a play.

There are many ways to give a play. One way is to make up the action and the dialogue as you act out the story.

Let's suppose you are giving a play about Christopher Columbus, and you are playing Columbus. You can make up your own lines, or dialogue, as you act out the play. You can make up your own pantomime, too. All the other actors will also make up their own dialogue and actions. You will not know exactly what each actor is going to say until he says it.

You will have to listen and to think quickly before you answer! It is an exciting way to do a play.

Often you will change your dialogue a little each time you practice, or *rehearse*, the play. You will think of new things to say to make a play come alive. The play will get more and more exciting.

But there is an important thing to remember. When you act out a play, you must know the character you are playing. You must do and say only what that character would do or say. Each character must seem real and alive to the audience.

COLUMBUS (*waving his sword triumphantly*):
  I have discovered America!

INDIAN CHIEF (*bowing low*):
  Welcome to America, brave Admiral.

Is this the way you would act out the story of Columbus? Christopher Columbus never knew he had discovered America. The Indian could not speak to Columbus in words for he did not know his language.

The Traveling Actors of Italy

IT IS FUN to make up the dialogue and story as you act out a play. We do it today and, hundreds of years ago, during the Renaissance in Italy, bands of traveling actors gave plays in this way, too.

At that time there were many beautiful theaters in Italy. Many were in the gardens of the noblemen. But the traveling actors did not give their plays for the nobles. They set up a wooden platform in a public square or at the side of the road and acted their plays for the people passing by.

These actors did not write out their plays. They used the same characters in each play, and they made up the story and dialogue as they acted out the play.

Most of their plays were comedies to make the people laugh. The people liked the plays so much that the traveling actors went all over Europe acting them. Soon people in other countries were acting these plays, too. But just like folk songs, the plays changed as they were acted in different countries and by different people.

Some of the funniest characters in the plays were called Harlequin and Punchinello and Columbina. When the plays were acted in France, the names changed to Pierrot and Columbine. The story of the plays changed, too. When the plays were acted in England, the names changed to Punch and Judy, and again the story of the plays changed. Today there are still Punch and Judy shows at English fairs, and people still like the plays and laugh at them.

Who Makes a Play?

LIKE the Italian actors, you can make up the action and dialogue of a play as you act it out. There are also other ways to give a play.

You can make up a play of your own or a play from history or from a favorite book. You can write out the action and the dialogue. Then you and the other actors can learn them by heart and act out the play.

Most often, you will act out a play somebody else has written. For like music, a play is created by many people.

There is the writer of the play. He is called the *playwright*. He writes about things he knows and remembers and imagines. He writes about things he thinks and feels, and the play tells much about him.

Often it tells where and when he lived. For like art and music, plays change as the way people work and play and live changes.

William Shakespeare lived in the days of the first Queen Elizabeth of England. Sometimes he wrote plays about the way the people of his time lived. Other times he wrote historical plays. But even when he wrote plays about history, Shakespeare told much about the way the people of his time felt and thought.

Today it is still exciting to see a play he wrote acted on the stage. The way the people talk and live is strange to us, but the way they feel is not strange. All through the ages people have had much the same hopes and fears.

The Folger Shakespeare Library

Shakespeare wrote *Macbeth* and *Romeo and Juliet* and other plays hundreds of years ago. Today they are still acted all over the world.

A playwright writes a play. The actors act it out.

Did you ever wonder how William Shakespeare would feel if he came back to earth today to watch his plays being acted? Do you think that his plays are acted in exactly the same way as they were when he was alive?

A playwright can write a play, but it is the actors who make it come alive on the stage. Like artists and musicians, actors are always trying and learning new ways to do things. The way they act out a play keeps changing as the way we work and play keeps changing.

There is another thing, too. An actor plays a character in a different way if he is playing on the stage or in a movie or on television. A stage is far away from the audience. You cannot see an actor's face close up as you can on a movie or television screen. Can you see why an actor must act differently for each?

Like painters and musicians, no two actors ever see the same thing in just the same way. Each actor has his own way of understanding a story character and acting him out. You may see the same play many times, and each time it will be a little different.

That is why a play is always new and exciting.

These actors are playing Romeo and Juliet on a stage.

These actors are playing Romeo and Juliet on television. Can you see why they have to act out the play differently?

151

The playwright writes a play. The actors act it out.

Who else helps create a play?

If you give a play in school, there is usually a teacher to help you plan it and pick the best player for each character part. Then she shows your class how to act out the play.

In a play on the stage, there is a person to do this, too. He is called the *director*.

The director chooses the actors to play the characters in the play. Each actor has his own way of acting out a character. The director knows this. But he knows, too, that there are many characters in a play. No one character can make the play come alive. No one actor can make the play come alive. The director thinks of the whole play. He helps the actors to work together to act out the play in the best way to make the play come alive.

The director also thinks of the playwright who wrote the play. He tries to help the actors act out the play in the way that he thinks the playwright wanted it acted.

Each actor has his own way of understanding a story character. Each director has his own way of understanding a play and directing it.

The playwright and the actors and the director all help create a play. Many other people also help in its production.

Artists, called *stage designers,* plan the stage setting and help create it.

Other artists plan and design the costumes for a play.

Other people make the costumes. Still others take care of them.

There are people who take care of the stage properties, too.

Carpenters build the stage sets.

Stagehands move the scenery on and off the stage.

Electricians take care of the lighting for a play. They use lights of different colors to show moonlight or sunlight or twilight. They use lights to make one part of the stage very bright while another part is in shadow.

Like the carpenters and the stagehands, they help carry out the stage designer's plan for the setting of the play.

On this page, you can see some of these people at work, getting ready for the actors.

Who else helps create a play?

We do as we sit and watch. We are the audience, and we help the play come alive for the actors and the others.

A Play with Music

MANY people work together to create a play, and there are many kinds of plays. You can act out a story in pantomime alone or with action and dialogue. You can also act out a story with music.

You can sing the dialogue instead of speaking the words. Then it will be an opera. You can dance the story in a ballet. You can act out the story with singing and dancing in an operetta or in a musical comedy.

Each way of giving a play is exciting. Each way is right for telling a certain kind of story.

Next time you give a play, try acting it out in different ways.

Sing the play as an opera. Did you ever see the opera *Pagliacci*? It is the story of an unhappy Punchinello and Columbina. Does that remind you of a play given by the Italian street actors?

Dance the story of the play.

Act out the story with singing and dancing in an operetta or a musical comedy.

Which way was best for your story?

It is exciting to try new ways of giving a play just as it is exciting to try new ways of painting a picture or singing a song.

Shadow Plays

IT IS exciting to act out stories in pantomime or in plays. It is exciting, too, to give a play with actors that are not people.

Did you ever show a shadow on a wall to make a rabbit or a squirrel? It is fun to see what shapes you can make with your fingers or hand.

It is even more fun to give a shadow play. You can take black construction paper or cardboard and cut out animals or human figures. We call these *silhouettes*.

Each figure must be exactly the right size. If you make a rabbit, it should not be bigger than the elephant you make! Tape your silhouette to an old coat hanger that you have straightened out and bent up at a right angle about two inches from one end.

You can cut out silhouettes for stage scenery, too, and attach them to a screen. You can make the screen from an old bedsheet or a white window shade and thumbtack it firmly to a frame. The screen is your shadow stage.

Be sure you have a strong, bright light—like an unshaded lamp —behind your shadow stage.

Now you are ready to act out your shadow play!

You can give any kind of shadow play you like. Just like a play with people, it will tell a story in action and dialogue. The shadows will be the actors as you move them.

But who will speak for the shadow actors? You can speak as you move them. You can make up the dialogue as you act out the story.

Sometimes you may want to write out the dialogue. Then you can move the shadows and somebody else can talk for them. You can give a shadow play any way you choose, but it is always fun!

157

Puppets . . .

SHADOWS are not the only actors that are not people.

You can give a play with a little doll-like figure you can wear on your fingers or hand. These are called hand puppets.

Did you ever watch a puppet play on television? The funny puppet can shake its head or nod. It can open its mouth and seem to talk.

It is easy to make a hand puppet. All you need is an old sock, some cotton batting, and a bit of paint. And you can make a funny kangaroo or a ferocious dragon or a sailor or a clown. You can make any kind of figure you choose.

Who talks for the puppet in a puppet show? You do. But the little puppet seems so real that you almost forget you are doing it. And sometimes you are surprised at the words you say for you are not speaking for yourself. You are speaking for the puppet. It is the actor.

Try a puppet play!

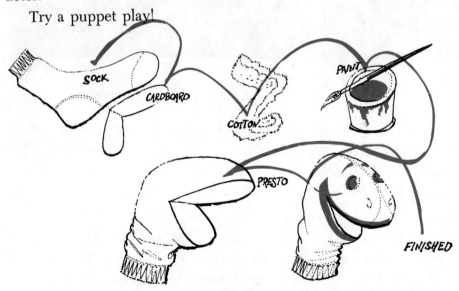

. . . and Marionettes

YOU can give a marionette play, too. A marionette is a doll that has wires or strings attached to it. By pulling the strings, you can make its legs and arms and head move. You can make it walk and sit and smile. Some marionettes can even turn somersaults and dance when you pull their strings.

A marionette is harder to make and to work than a hand puppet. But people have made marionettes and loved them for hundreds of years in countries all over the world.

It is exciting to act out a play with real people. But sometimes it is even more exciting to give a puppet or marionette play.

Sometimes we find it hard to act in a play. We stumble over words or feel shy. It is different in a puppet or marionette play. We speak for the puppets and the marionettes, but they are the actors. They come alive as we move them. We do not feel shy, for we are only the voices. The marionettes and puppets are giving the play.

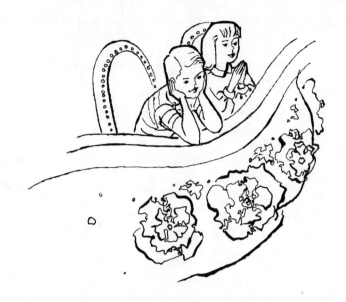

The World Is a Stage

THERE are many kinds of plays and many kinds of actors—people and shadows, puppets and marionettes. We can give a play in our own back yard or at school or in church or in a community building. We can watch a play in a theater building or in an outdoor theater. We can watch a play, too, in the movies or on television. We can listen to a play on radio.

Always a play takes us on a journey into the wonderful make-believe world of the imagination. We can travel backward and forward in time and see how people lived long ago and how they may live in the future. We can visit lands all around the world and see how people live and work and play in every country under the sun.

As we watch a play being performed the story characters help us understand our real world. We learn to know something of why people do the things they do. We learn to know, too, why we sometimes do the things we do.

As we learn this we grow to understand that people everywhere, in every time and every country, are much alike. We learn to make friends all over the world.

Art *AND THE WORLD AROUND US*

Look and Listen!

IF WE use our eyes to look and see and our ears to listen and hear, there are shapes and colors and sounds all around us. Artists of many kinds have created them. Each tells us a story.

A shadow on the sidewalk has a shape. Sometimes it is as tall as a giant. Sometimes it is short and squat. A tree and a boy and a kitten playing with its tail cast different kinds of shadows. A shadow shape changes as the sunlight changes. What kind of story does a shadow shape tell?

Trees have shapes. Many have colors that change as the seasons change. The rustling of their leaves in the springtime and summer makes one kind of music. The howling of the wind through their bare branches in winter makes another kind of music.

Some shapes and colors and sounds belong to the country. Others are part of a town or a city. Everywhere we go, we see things that tell where we live and how we live. They make pictures of the world of today.

We hear sounds, too, that tell us about the way we live. A school bell rings. A plane roars overhead. A cow moos in a meadow. The sounds of the country and the town and the city make a kind of symphony of life today.

Pantomimes and dramatic plays are all around us. A girl runs down the street after a school bus. Without speaking a word, she acts out a story. A boy milks a cow, and the cow kicks the milk pail over. Will the boy laugh or be angry? A story is in the making.

Art and music and drama are part of our daily lives. All through the ages, artists of many kinds have used these sounds and colors and shapes to express what they see and hear and feel and imagine.

163

All the arts tell a story or express a feeling or a thought or stir us with the beauty of shapes and colors and sounds. Often it is difficult to tell where one art begins and another ends, for many arts and artists work together.

When you hear the music of a band, your feet begin to tap and you start to sway to the rhythm. Are you dancing or are you acting out a pantomime?

The music does not always come first. Often you start to tap out a dance beat and find you are whistling a tune. For music and dancing belong together.

When you listen to the music of a symphony orchestra, often pictures are created in your mind. Sometimes they are the pictures the composer saw when he wrote the music. Other times you create pictures of your own. But it is the music that inspires the pictures you see.

How many arts are used in a play? A playwright writes the play. Actors act it out through dialogue and pantomime. Artists create the costumes, the scenery, and the setting.

In an opera, music helps tell the story. In an operetta and a musical comedy, music and dancing help tell the story.

No art is separate. Artists work with many different tools and in many different ways, but always they help us share the things they know and think and feel and imagine. Always they help us grow in understanding of ourselves and of the world around us.

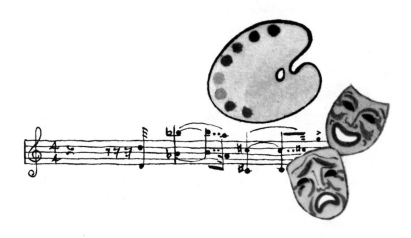

Art and the Way We Live

A PAINTING and a statue in a museum are art. A play upon a stage and a song over the radio are forms of art. But there are many other kinds of art, and they are part of the way we live.

How many kinds of art can you find as you walk down a street? Look! There is a giant billboard advertisement. The picture tells a story that creates a feeling that makes you want to buy what it is selling.

You can see advertisements in newspapers and magazines and many other places, too. Some are pictures an artist draws or paints. Others are photographs. A photographer uses a camera to create a picture of sunlight and shadows, colors and shapes.

Some advertisements are singing commercials on radio. Others are quick dramatic plays on television. Advertising artists use art and music and drama to tell their stories.

There are many different kinds of advertisements, for they sell many different kinds of things to many different kinds of people. What kind of advertisements do you like? Do they sell pumpkin pies or baseball bats, shoes or automobiles, puppies or school books?

There is an advertisement for almost everything we eat or wear or use.

Each advertisement is part of the way we live. Each tells much about how we live.

165

A fashion designer sketches a design.

.She cuts out a dress pattern from muslin.

She pins the muslin pattern on a model to see how her design will really look. Then a dressmaker makes the dress.

The Clothes We Wear

THE CLOTHES we wear are part of the way we live, too. An Eskimo boy of the frozen north dresses differently from a boy who lives on the hot sands of the Sahara desert. A girl of today dresses differently from a girl who lived when George Washington was President.

Like costumes in a play, the clothes we wear tell a story. Often they tell where we live. They tell much about how we live and work and play.

Clothes help us keep warm when it is cold. They help us feel cool when it is hot. They help us keep dry when it is raining. We wear different kinds of clothes when we go to school or to a party, when we swim or ride horseback.

Clothes help us in another way. Long ago when a cave man killed an animal, he wore its skin proudly for it showed he was a mighty hunter. Today we still like to wear clothes that help us feel proud and happy. We like to wear clothes that make us look and feel attractive.

There are artists who help us do this, for they create the styles of the clothes we wear. We call these artists *fashion designers*.

Some fashion designers are men. Many others are women. Like a painter, a fashion designer works with colors and shapes. She works, too, with materials of many kinds — silks and cottons, furs and wools, leathers and plastics, and many others.

A fashion designer creates a kind of picture — and you are part of the picture. For she creates the style of the suit or dress, the shoes and hat, and everything you wear.

A tall boy needs a different kind of style than a short boy. A thin girl needs a different kind of style than a chubby girl. The fashion designer creates different kinds of styles to help each of us look attractive.

Which is the right style for you?

What does this room tell you about the boy who lives in it?

The Rooms We Live In

THE CLOTHES people wear tell much about them. The way a room looks tells other things. Usually we plan the way our own room looks. Some people plan, or design, rooms for others. These people are called *interior decorators*. Like all artists, they make a plan, or design, and carry it out with shapes and colors and materials of different kinds.

Let's pretend you are seeing your room for the first time. What do you see? Is it big and square or long and narrow? Is it light and airy? Where are the windows? Where are the lamps? Are they in the right place to give you the best light when you read or study? What pictures are on the wall and where are they placed? What colors are the wallpaper and the rug and the spread on your bed?

How does the room make you feel when you look at it? Does it give you a happy feeling?

An interior decorator thinks of all these things when he designs a room. He tries to see the room as a whole so that everything in it fits together. He plans the colors and materials to use and where the furniture should be placed.

An interior decorator thinks of how a room will be used. A kitchen and a living room and a bedroom need different things in them.

He thinks, too, of the people who will use the rooms he designs. He knows that each person is different. Each person needs different things around him.

Like a stage setting, a room tells a story about the person who lives in it. A girl's room will be different from a boy's room. A baby's room will be different from a teen-ager's room.

What story does your room tell about you? Do you like to collect horse pictures or baseball pictures? Do you like to build model planes or rockets? Your room will tell that.

If you were an interior decorator what changes would you make in your room? It is fun to plan and arrange a room the way you want it to look, and often all it takes is a little imagination.

What does this room tell you about the boy who lives in it?

The Art of Handicraft

CAN you remember the first time you carved a set of wooden book ends or wove a basket? Did you know you were practicing one of the oldest arts in the world — the art of handicraft?

For thousands and thousands of years, people have been making things with their hands or with simple hand tools. That is why this art is called *handicraft*.

Long before written history began, the people who lived in caves made stone axes and hatchets. At first they did not care how these tools looked. They just wanted them to be useful. But later, they began shaping tools that were graceful as well as strong. When they made a harpoon, they carved a reindeer or other animal on it. Then cave men who lived at a later time began weaving baskets and decorating them with patterns. They used the baskets to hold food and other things. They made pottery and decorated it with designs of lines or zigzags or dots.

That was the beginning of handicraft as an art. Ever since then, in countries all over the world, people have been carving and weaving and molding pottery and shaping bronze and silver into shapes of their own design.

Like painting and music and drama, handicraft tells much about the artist who created it and when and where and how he lived.

Before the invention of machinery, everything people used had to be made by the hands or with simple hand tools. Each person worked alone or with a few helpers. Each thing was made separately, and no two things ever came out exactly alike.

A woman sat at her loom and wove the cloth for the clothing her family wore. She wove the blankets and spreads for the bed and the rug for the floor. Often as she wove, she created her own designs.

In medieval times, a queen wove, too, and directed her ladies in waiting in weaving. The stone castle walls were cold, and so often coverings were woven to hang on the walls and make the room warmer. Often these coverings, or *tapestries*, were decorated with patterns or with pictures woven into them.

New York State Museum and Science Service

Huskface Mask

This Huskface mask was used
by Seneca Indians of western
New York state in religious
ceremonies. Do you see
how handicraft reflects the
way people live?

Chicago Natural History Museum

Ceremonial Bowl

This bowl was used by the Aztec Indians
of Mexico in their religious ceremonies.
The animal carved in stone is an ocelot,
a large member of the cat family.

The Bayeux Tapestry

Tradition tells us that about 900 years ago Queen Matilda and her ladies
embroidered this tapestry to tell the story of the king, William
the Conqueror. The pictures were made with colored threads on linen.

171

The World of the Arts

Clay Pitcher
(1370 A.D.–1520 A.D.) Aztec

This clay pitcher was made and decorated
by an Indian artist in Mexico long ago.
Do you see how he has used curves to make
a pattern?

Paul Revere in His Workshop   **Silver Coffee Pot**
Paul Revere (1735–1818) American

Paul Revere created many beautiful designs in his workshop. A design
for silver is different from a pottery design. Like a sculptor, a handicraft artist
uses different tools and materials to make different kinds of designs.

Until the invention of machinery, pottery, too, was made by one
man working alone or with helpers. Some potters shaped the clay by
hand to make a pot or pitcher or jar. Other potters shaped the clay
on a potter's wheel. Often potters created shapes of their own design
and decorated them with their own patterns. These designs and
decorations help tell us when and where a potter lived.

Silversmiths, too, worked alone or with helpers as they shaped
vessels of silver. They, too, often created their own designs and
decorations. One of the famous silversmiths of colonial America was
the American patriot Paul Revere. Did you ever read the poem by
Henry Wadsworth Longfellow called *Paul Revere's Ride?*

There are many forms of handicraft and many kinds of handicraft artists. Handicraft may be a chair or a cup, a sword or an enameled locket. It may be a bedspread or a glass goblet. It may be a carved jewel box or a silver salt cellar or many other things we use.

Once all the things people used were made by hand. Today most of the things we use are made by machinery. Thousands of articles are made from one design. We call this *mass production*. It is a quick and economical way to make things. Today we buy most of the things we need and use. But there are still handicraft artists who weave and carve, mold pottery and shape metal to designs they create. It is exciting to create a design and make it yourself with your hands.

Chicago Natural History Museum

Wooden Seat
(?) Inca

The handicraft artist who made this large wooden seat lived long ago in Cuzco, Peru. What story does the design he carved and painted tell you?

The Gunsmith's Shop
Woodcut, 1842

A gunsmith made musket rifles, pistols, and other firearms. Does this remind you of a factory today?

Head of War Club
(19th Century) Brazil

An Indian who lived in Brazil during the nineteenth century made this head for a war club. Do you think he worked in a shop like the gunsmith did?

The Industrial Arts

TODAY we live in a world of machines and mass production. New arts have arisen because of this. These are called *industrial arts,* for they are part of the way we work.

The handicraft artist creates an object by himself. The industrial artist, or *designer*, creates designs that are made by machinery through mass production.

Did you ever wonder how you would design a car? You can draw a picture of a car on paper. That is easy. But will the car be strong and swift and safe to drive? Will it be easy to drive and comfortable to ride in? What materials will you use to make it so? Will machines be able to make the car quickly and cheaply from the design?

The industrial designer must know the answers to all these questions. He must know about materials and always keep trying to find new ways of using them. Each material is different. Wood and steel and plastic look different and are strong in different ways. Glass and paper and rubber take different shapes and are useful for different things.

The industrial designer must also know about machinery, for his designs will be produced by machines. His designs must make it easy for the machines to turn out thousands of cars or other objects swiftly and well.

The industrial designer must know, too, what actions people make as they work and play. He must fit his designs to match the actions. Then the object he helps create will be easy for people to use.

When mass production began, there were no industrial designers. The kinds of designs handicraft artists created were used. But as industrial art grew, artists began to realize that machine-made objects needed a different kind of design than handicraft did.

Today many industrial artists are trying new ways to make designs that are right for machines. They are creating designs that are beautifully simple and strong and that machines can reproduce easily. They are helping create objects that people can use easily, too. The industrial arts tell much about the changing way we live.

The way we live is always
changing as people try
new ways and new ideas.

Bettmann Archive

Bettmann Archive

This house is very old. It was built in Salem, Massachusetts, about 1662.
Do you think the builder remembered a house he knew when he planned it? Often people built houses like the ones they lived in and loved when they were young.

This house in the French Quarter of New Orleans was built in 1863. Do you see the lacy pattern of the iron balconies? If you did not know it was in New Orleans, would you think this was a house for a cold climate? A warm climate?

Art and Architects

THE CUPS and saucers, the tables and chairs in our houses are designed by handicraft artists or industrial designers. Did you ever think of your house as a design, too?

In the days of the pioneers, men went into the wilderness and cut down trees and built their own houses. They used the materials they found around them to build sturdy shelters against snow and wind and rain. Often they built their houses as protection against enemy Indians, too. Usually they did not think of the way the house looked.

Today an artist called an *architect* designs a house. He, too, thinks of strength and safety. He uses old and new ideas and materials to make the house light and airy, warm in winter and cool in summer.

But he thinks of more than this. He knows that people want more than shelter from their houses. They want beauty and grace around them. They want homes that reflect the way they live.

176

The architect thinks of a house as a design. The way the house looks inside is part of the design. The outside of the house is also part of the design.

The architect knows, too, that a house does not stand alone. It is part of the countryside or of the city around it. He plans one kind of house for a hilltop and another kind for a seashore and still another kind of house for a city street.

He thinks about climate, too. A house for a very hot climate and a house for a very cold climate will need different designs.

An architect asks many questions as he plans a house, but always he remembers one important thing. A house is for people. Who will live in the house he is designing?

Will it be an apartment building where many families live or will it be a house for just one family?

How much money can the people spend to build the house?

What kind of family will live in it? Will there be small children? Then the architect must plan space for them to play in and space for them to grow in. Families grow in size, too, and the architect must plan for this as he designs a house.

What do the people like to do? Do they like to read or play music or play games? An architect tries to fit his design to the people who will live in the house.

The famous American architect Frank Lloyd Wright designed this house. It is called 'Falling Water.' Do you see how it seems to be part of the landscape?

177

Bettmann Archive

Bettmann Archive

St. Paul's Cathedral

Sir Christopher Wren designed this famous cathedral in London, England. It was built in 1675-1710. All through the ages, people have built places of worship. Do you see how he used different kinds of shapes in his design?

An architect designs homes. He also designs schools and churches, hospitals and libraries, factories and office buildings, and many other kinds of buildings.

Like a sculptor, an architect creates a form that has shapes and thickness. You can walk around a sculptured figure or a building. You can touch the roughness of stone or brick or the cool smoothness of marble.

A sculptor molds or carves or shapes his figure. An architect creates a design that other men will build with stone and glass and brick and wood and steel and many other materials. Both are artists.

Architects design many kinds of buildings. Each building is used in a different way. Architects use many shapes and materials in creating their designs, but always they try to fit the shapes and materials to the way the building will be used.

Like art and music and drama, the buildings around us reflect the ways we live.

Santa Fe Railway Photo

Football Stadium, Rice Institute

This large stadium is in Houston, Texas.
Its design is very different
from the skyscraper.
It, too, reflects the way we live.

Pan American World Airways Photo

Palace of Dawn

The Palace of Dawn in Brasilia is the
home of the president of Brazil. Does it
remind you of our White House in
Washington? Like other artists,
architects like to try using shapes and
materials in new ways.

Arts and Architecture Magazine

The Seagram Building

This skyscraper towers to the
sky in New York City.
Many busy people work in it.
Do you see how strong and
uncluttered its design is?

179

An architect designs a building, but he does not build it. Who builds a home or school or church or other building?

Many people work together to do this. We rarely think of these people as artists, yet they help create the building. Each has a special kind of work to do. Without this work, there would be no home or school or church or skyscraper.

How many parts does a building have? There are some you can see. There are some you cannot see, but they help make the building strong and safe and ready for you to live and work and play in.

You cannot see the foundation, for it is under the building. Workers dig the foundation. They strengthen it with concrete or wood or steel or other materials. They know the foundation must be strong, for it helps support the weight of the building and all the things and people in it.

Other workers erect the girders and beams and columns. Like the bones of a body, these help the building stand up straight and strong.

Workers put up the roof and outer walls of the building. Other workers put up the inside walls and the ceilings.

Carpenters put in doors and windows. They put catches on the windows and locks on the doors and many other things.

Electricians install electric-outlet boxes and other things we need to give us lights and electricity for toasters and television sets and other things we use.

Plumbers put in pipes for gas and water and sewage. They put in the bathrooms and kitchen and laundry equipment.

Workers install equipment to give us heat. They put in the refrigerators and air-conditioning units, too.

Painters paint the inside of the building. They paint the outside of the building, too.

All these and many other kinds of workers help create the buildings we live and work in. They help create the libraries and museums and hospitals. They help carry out the design of the architect.

There is another important worker who helps create the building.

He is the contractor. He hires the people who work on the building. He buys the materials they use. He and the workers and the architect build the homes and schools and churches together.

All these workers help carry out
the design of a building.

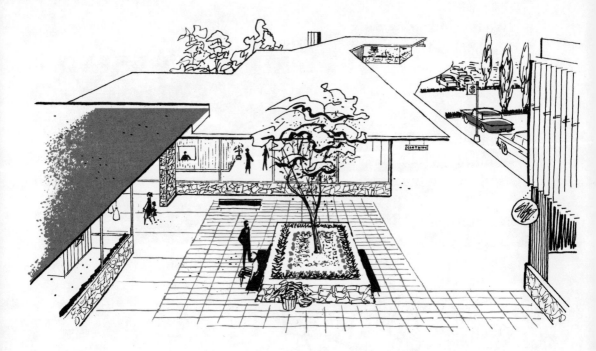

The Towns We Live In

Y OUR TOWN makes a kind of design, too. Houses and schools and churches and other buildings make shapes against the sky. Trees and parks make shapes, too. Streets make straight or curved lines.

It is like a design for a stage setting, and the people in the town are the actors on the stage. Traffic hums on busy streets. Men and women work in homes and stores, offices and factories. Boys and girls work and play. Daily dramas are everywhere.

Many people plan and work together to make a town or city a safe and busy and pleasant place to live. Usually we do not think of these people as artists, yet they create the design for the towns we live in.

They can plan schools and libraries and hospitals. They can plan parks and playgrounds, too. They can plan streets that are wide and smooth so traffic will flow swiftly and safely, and they can plant trees to shade the streets.

They can also plan convenient shopping centers and parking lots. They can pave the parking lots and decorate them with shrubbery, for they know that stores are busier when shopping is made pleasant.

We do not know when people first started planning cities. Probably it was thousands of years ago. Ancient Athens, in Greece, was built on a high hill to make it easy to defend against enemies. In medieval times, cities were built around a central market place. Walls were built around the city to keep it safe. All the people lived inside these walls. As the city grew, it became crowded. Some people began settling outside the walls. The city had outgrown its plan.

Later people forgot a city had to have a plan. Cities just grew and grew. We still have cities like these. Buildings are crowded together. Traffic crowds the streets. There is little space to park a car.

Neighborhoods change as a city becomes crowded. A street of pleasant homes and gardens often turns into a street of smoky factories and dilapidated houses. Because there are not enough houses, poor people who live in these run-down neighborhoods are crowded together.

When too many people live in one place, it becomes dirty and unhealthy. Children who live there do not get enough air and sunshine to help them grow strong and healthy.

Today city planners are trying to make over these run-down neighborhoods. They are trying to provide pleasant and healthy places for people to live and work and play. They tear down old buildings and build new ones. They fix up old buildings.

They try to leave space for sunshine and trees and fresh air.

They know that disease can spread from one section of a city to another. Unhappiness and ill health can cause crime, and crime can spread, too. The city planners know that a city is only as healthy as all of its people.

Like artists, city planners are trying to design our cities to reflect the changing ways we live.

Old South Meeting House
Boston, Massachusetts

Boston is often called the "Cradle of Liberty" for many of the stirring events of the American Revolution happened there. Do you remember reading about the Boston Tea Party? It was planned in this meeting house in Boston.

While city planners try to change old towns and cities to make them safer and healthier places in which to live, they also try to keep some things unchanged.

They know that each city, like each person, is just a little different from every other city. Each city reflects the way the people in it live today.

Many cities also tell the story of how people in years past lived in them. Many cities help tell the history of a country.

City planners try to keep old buildings that are part of our country's history.

In the Old North Church in Boston, the lanterns were hung that sent Paul Revere on his famous ride to warn the Minute Men of the American Revolution that the British redcoats were coming.

Mount Vernon in Virginia was the home of our first president, George Washington.

Abraham Lincoln's house in Springfield, Illinois, still stands.

When we visit these historic places, we remember the great men who helped build our nation. The history of our country comes alive for us.

We are inspired to do our part to keep our country strong and brave and free.

Some historic buildings are now used as museums to show how people lived long ago.

Other ancient buildings are still used as they were when they were first built.

Some churches are centuries old, but people still worship in them. Trinity Church in New York City is one of these. In it, we can still see the pew in which George Washington sat.

Some schools are hundreds of years old. One of these schools is Eton College in England.

Eton is not a college as we in our country think of a college. It is one of the largest private schools for boys in England and stands on the east bank of the Thames River. It was founded by King Henry VI in 1440. Many famous Englishmen went to school there, and boys still study there today.

Some homes, too, are hundreds of years old, but people still live in them.

As you walk down a city street, often you can see an ancient building and a towering skyscraper side by side. Both help tell the story of a city and its people. Both are part of the picture of a city.

Both reflect the way a city grows and changes as the way the people live changes.

Trinity Church, New York City

George Washington worshipped in this famous old church that stands at the head of Wall Street in New York City. Near it a skyscraper towers to the sky. Many people work in the skyscraper. Many people worship in the church. Together, these old and new buildings help create a picture of New York City and its people.

185

Street Scene
Canterbury, England

This street in Canterbury is very different from a busy traffic center in New York City, but both reflect the way people live.

British Information Services

British Information Services

English Village
Essex, England

This country village in England is different from the great city of London, but both are part of England.

A city and a town and a small village are different in many ways, but they are also alike in some ways. Each has homes and schools and churches. Each has places where people work and play. Each reflects the way the people in it live.

Each helps tell the story of its country. Each is a part of the picture of its country.

New York City is part of the United States, but it is not the whole picture of the United States. A fishing village in Maine is part of the picture, too. A cattle town in the west is also a part of the picture. Together, they — and many other cities and towns and villages — create the picture of our country.

England and France, India and Japan, and other countries around the world each has cities and towns and villages. Like our cities, and towns, and villages, these help create a picture of the country.

186

Who are the people who plan for a village or a town or a city? The people who govern a village plan for it. They try to fit their plan to the way the people in the village live.

The people who govern a town or a city also help plan for the town or city and try to fit the plan to the way the people live.

There are many others who help plan for a village, a town, and a city. The people on the school and hospital boards are some of these planners. Your own mother and father also help create the design for the place where you live. They do this when they vote for the people who govern the village or town or city.

You, too, help create the picture of the place where you live. The way you act at home and at school and on the playground is part of the picture. The way you act when you meet friends or strangers is another part of the picture.

As you help create a picture of the town in which you live, you also create a picture of your country. For each village and town and city is part of the picture a country presents to the world.

Philip Gendreau

Skyline, New York City

New York City is different from either London or Paris, but each city helps tell the story of its country. Each helps create a picture of its country.

187

The Way We Travel

MAN, the builder, creates many shapes and forms. Like a painting and a song and a play, these reflect the changing ways we live. Man builds homes and towns and cities. He builds roads, too, to link these together. Over these roads, men travel.

Did you ever think of a road as a picture? It has straight or curved lines. It can run flat and straight between fields of grain. It can climb a hill or twist around the winding curve of a mountain.

Like a painting, a road tells a story. It tells us where it is. A country lane is different from a city street. A wide highway where many cars travel is different from a narrow mountain pass.

It tells us when it was built. Sometimes it tells us who built it. One of the most famous roads in the world was built by the ancient Romans. It is called the Appian Way, and it runs from Rome to the southeast coast of Italy. It was begun in 312 B.C., and it took three hundred years to complete. Part of this great stone road still stands today.

A road tells us much about the way the people who use it live. Before the invention of automobiles, people traveled on foot or on horseback. They drove wagons or carts or stagecoaches drawn by horses. Today we drive cars swiftly from place to place. We build wide, strong highways for the cars to travel on.

Like the people who design our homes and the people who plan our cities, our highway builders are kinds of artists, too.

They work with surveying tools and cement and concrete and many other kinds of materials. They try to make our highways strong and safe for cars to travel on swiftly.

They divide the highways into lanes. Cars in some lanes travel in one direction. Cars in other lanes travel in the opposite direction. This lessens the danger of cars colliding. They plan highways where there are few crossroads so cars can drive for hundred of miles without a stop. This, too, helps make the highways safe.

Often they plant grass and trees beside the highways to make them beautiful as well as swift and safe for travelers.

The Appian Way

Editors Digest

This highway was built by the ancient Romans before the birth of Christ. Although the buildings along the road have crumbled with age, parts of the highway are still used today.

Cloverleaf Intersection

Exxon

This picture was taken from a plane flying over the intersection of two highways in New Jersey. The design permits cars to move quickly and safely from one highway to the other.

Photo by Underwood & Underwood

International Peace Bridge, Buffalo, New York

This bridge links Buffalo, New York, and Fort Erie, Ontario. It symbolizes
the friendship between the people of the United States and Canada.

The way we travel helps tell the story of the changing ways we
live. It helps create a picture of the world we live in.

Wide highways link our cities from coast to coast. Bridges span
wide rivers and deep canyons. Airports and rocket towers tell the
story that today man has planes that can fly swiftly across continents
and oceans. Man has built rockets that can zoom into space.

The people who design and build the highways and bridges are
also artists. They work with shapes and forms and materials of
many kinds.

The people who design and build the planes and rockets are kinds
of artists, too. They create shapes that move. These moving shapes
create sounds that are part of the pattern of the way we live.

The shapes they build tell a story without words. They tell the
story that people and freight and ideas are moving all around the
world of today.

190

U. S. Army Photo

Juno II and the Boom Catcher

These shapes are part of the picture of the world of today. Rockets zoom into the sky. They launch satellites into orbit. Men have begun the exploration of space.

U. S. Army Photo

Dulles Air Terminal, Washington, D.C.

The architect used sweeping lines to create the feeling of motion and flight. He wanted the building to remind travelers of the speed and grace of modern jet airliners.

191